MW00624515

THE REISS
MOTIVATION
PROFILE®

THE REISS MOTIVATION PROFILE®

What Motivates You?

STEVEN REISS, PH.D.

The Reiss Motivation Profile®: What Motivates You? Steven Reiss, Ph.D.

© 2013 IDS PUBLISHING CORPORATION
P.O. Box 389
Worthington, Ohio 43085

All rights reserved. No part of this book may be reproduced in any form or by any means, electronic or mechanical, including photocopying, recording, or by any information storage and retrieval system, without permission in writing from the publisher.

LIBRARY OF CONGRESS CATALOGING-IN-PUBLICATION DATA

Reiss, Steven
Reiss motivation profile: What motivates you?: psychology, social science/Steven Reiss.--1st pbk. ed.

This book is based on material that was previously peer reviewed.

ISBN 978-0-9891701-1-6

Cover and Interior Design: AuthorSupport.com

Dedication

On July 5, 2011, I was rushed to the Ohio State University Medical Center. When I regained consciousness in the ER, I noticed that my shirt was drenched in blood. The attending doctor told me that my hemoglobin was only 3.3, which is far below the minimum level needed to sustain life. I was sent to intensive care.

After a week of futile effort to locate the internal source of the bleed, my doctors told my wife, Maggi, and my adult children, Mike and Ben, that they had done everything they could to locate the bleeding, couldn't find it, and I would die in an hour or so. Maggi begged the doctors to return to the procedure room and resume their search. Shortly thereafter they found an artery in my liver gushing out blood. That evening Dr. Hooman Khabiri, an interventional radiologist, burned the artery, and it hasn't shed any blood since.

I was discharged from the hospital on July 30, 2011. This book was written in Jupiter, Florida in the winter months of 2013.

This Book is Dedicated to Maggi

Table of Contents

Table of Contents (continued)

The 16 Basic Desires of Human Nature

Acceptance, the desire for positive self-regard.

Curiosity, the desire for understanding.

Eating, the desire for food.

Family, the desire to raise children and spend time with siblings.

Honor, the desire for upright character.

Idealism, the desire for social justice.

Independence, the desire for self-reliance.

Order, the desire for structure.

Physical Activity, the desire for muscle exercise.

Power, the desire for influence or leadership.

Romance, the desire for beauty and sex.

Saving, the desire to collect.

Social Contact, the desire for peer companionship.

Status, the desire for respect based on social standing.

Tranquility, the desire for safety.

Vengeance, the desire to confront those who offend.

Seven Principles of Motivational Psychology

1. **Principle of Universal Goals.** *Certain goals are common to every-one and deeply rooted in human nature.* The motivation to experience these universal goals is called "intrinsic motivation" or "basic desire." Examples of universal goals include understanding, status, and structured environment. Reiss's list of 16 basic desires is the first scientifically derived and validated taxonomy of universal goals.

2. **Principle of Intrinsic Motivation.** *Intrinsic motives (basic desires) have two characteristics: what is desired, which is the universal in human motivation, and how much is typically desired, which is the particular in human motivation.* We all want the same things – acceptance, understanding, sustenance, offspring, character, justice, freedom, structure, exercise, competence, sex, preparedness, belonging, respect, safety, and victory -- but not to the same extent. Everybody embraces the 16 basic desires, but individuals prioritize them differently. How an individual prioritizes the 16 basic desires is called a "Reiss Motivation Profile®" or "Reiss Profile®. " It reveals personality traits and core values.

3. **Principle of Relationship Compatibility.** *People are naturally motivated to assert their basic desires in relationships.* Couples with similar desire profiles typically have shared values and bond. Those with dissimilar desire profiles typically have opposite values and quarrel.

4. **Principle of Strong Basic Desires.** *Strong basic desires motivate interest in multiple gratification objects.* People with hearty appe-

tites eat many different kinds of food; curious people are interested in learning about different topics; romantic people seek multiple partners.

5. **Principle of Counseling/ Coaching.** *A person thrives in relationships, work, and family situations that satisfy his or her most important basic desires.* Better to marry the right person to begin with than to need a counselor to learn to get along with your partner.

6. **Principle of Self-Hugging.** *We often think our values are best, not just for us, but for everyone.* We use the tactics of "everyday tyranny" to pressure others to change their priorities for ours, thinking it is for their own good. We are a naturally intolerant species.

7. **Principle of a Greater Motive.** *Personality change can occur only when the basic desire(s) motivating change is/are stronger than the one(s) motivating the current traits.* Often there are few or no such greater motives, or they cannot be practically applied. Hence personality change is difficult to accomplish.

Definitions of Terms Used in This Book

Term	Definition
basic desire	Same as intrinsic motivation. Consists of what is wanted, which is common to everyone, and how much, which depends on the individual's core values.
compound motive	Two or more basic desires acting in combination.
core value	Valuation or prioritization of a basic desire; typically determines the strength of a basic desire or psychological need.
greater motive	A basic desire with a very high valuation.
high (desire, need)	Valuing a basic desire at least 0.8 standard deviations above the norm. Same as "strong basic desire."
extrinsic motivation	In social psychology's re-statement of mind-body dualism, extrinsic motivation is variously defined as "tissue needs," coercion, materialism, or hedonism. The distinction between intrinsic-extrinsic motivation (mind-body dualism) is invalid.
everyday tyranny	Common efforts to change others to embrace one's own core values.

intrinsic motivation	Motivation to assert core values and the management of experiences with universal goals.
intrinsic motive	Basic desire, intrinsic motive, and psychological need are interchangeable terms.
low (need)	Valuing a basic desire at least 0.8 standard deviation below the norm. Same as "weak desire."
motive	Reason to initiate or maintain a behavior.
need	Basic desire, intrinsic motive, and psychological need are interchangeable terms.
personality trait	Well-practiced habits for managing one or more basic desires.
self-hugging	The presumption that one's core values potentially make other people happy.
Reiss Profile®	1. A standardized psychological questionnaire of intrinsic motives. Same as Reiss Motivation Profile®. 2. How an individual prioritizes the 16 basic desires.

PART I

Conceptual and Scientific Foundations

CHAPTER 1

The Pleasure Principle

An original and comprehensive new theory of human motivation —
called the theory of 16 basic desires — is presented in this book.
The theory expresses new ideas on the fundamental nature of human
motivation and how motives are connected to values, traits, and relationships. It meets the four scientific criteria of construct validity, measurement reliability, controlled observations, and verifiable implications.
This is an original theory that has significant scientific validity. It excels
in the prediction of how people will behave in natural environments and
in relationships.

The story of our work on 16 basic desires began in 1995 when I was
diagnosed with sclerosing cholangitis, which is a potentially fatal autoimmune disease of the liver ducts. In this disease the ducts in the liver

become inflamed every so often, leaving behind scar tissue that narrows them. This leads to life-threatening infections and gradually cirrhosis of the liver. The only treatment is liver transplantation, which I underwent in 2002. Sclerosing cholangitis is the disease that took the life of Chicago Bear football great Walter Payton.

I recall my personal experience because it led me to rethink what it is that makes my life meaningful, which in turn led to the research that is the subject of this book. Many research psychologists have assumed that human behavior is guided by the desire to feel good, or what I call the "Pleasure Principle". According to this principle, what people want above all is to maximize their pleasure and to minimize their pain. It implies that we can measure the quality of a person's life by determining the excess of positive over negative feelings.

The Pleasure Principle suggests that we can explain everything people do in terms of a calculus of pleasure and pain. It suggests that people prefer optimism to pessimism because optimism is the more pleasurable of the two outlooks. Similarly, people prefer movies with happy rather than sad endings, even when the happy endings are unrealistic. How does this principle explain the fact that many people work at boring jobs? It implies that working at such jobs is the lesser of two evils, predicting that people would dislike unemployment even more than they dislike their boring jobs.

Those who advocate the validity of the Pleasure Principle — variously called pleasure theorists or hedonists — say that nature uses pleasure and pain to prod us to do what is necessary for our health and survival. For example, nature uses hunger to tell us when we need to eat and thirst to signal when we need to drink. Since feeling hungry and thirsty are unpleasant, we are motivated to eat and drink, when it is essential for health and survival.

Many influential psychologists embraced the Pleasure Principle in one form or another. It has been suggested, for example, that Freud's construct of libido is basically a variant of this principle. The behaviorist view of motivation as reward and punishment is transparently similar to pleasure theory. Bernard Weiner (1995), a social psychologist, defined intrinsic motivation as pleasure inherent to the performance of certain behaviors.

So if everybody is maximizing pleasure and minimizing pain, why do workaholics spend little time relaxing, having fun with their families, or taking vacations? According to pleasure theory, it is because they enjoy their work and feel restless when away from it. Pleasure theorists argue that workaholics are really doing what for them maximizes positive feelings or minimizes negative feelings.

Is the desire to feel good all that motivates us? Are pleasure and pain the ultimate forces guiding our behavior? I answer negatively. In deciding how to proceed when faced with a life-threatening illness, I did not give much consideration to how much pain I might experience. Instead, I was guided by my love and responsibilities for my family. My aim was for good things to happen to my family, beyond benefits for me. Although parents take pleasure in their children's well being, that does not mean that parents help their children for the selfish benefit of experiencing the joys of parenthood.

One morning in the hospital I experimented by thinking of what people were doing solely in terms of the pleasure and pain it brought them. When the nurse came in to take my temperature, I wondered why she was not doing something that would bring her greater pleasure. If having fun and feeling good are the goals of all behavior, as pleasure theorists claim, who would want to work in a hospital? Hospitals are filled with people who are sick including some who are dying. In late mornings I could hear patients awake from surgery, screaming in pain. Since nurses have the ability to find some other place to work, why wouldn't they do so if their overdriving desire were to feel good?

The more I thought about the question, the more convinced I became that pleasure and pain do not drive our behavior to anywhere near the extent assumed by some psychologists. Pleasure is the byproduct of getting what we desire; it is not the aim of the desire. The goal of experiencing pleasure does not create the nurse's desire to help

If pleasure and pain do not drive our behavior, what does?

patients; rather, altruism prods nurses to make sacrifices for their patients, and when they do so, they experience pleasure. The goal of avoiding guilt does not create the soldier's desire to sacrifice for the good of his or her country; rather honor motivates soldiers to make sacrifices.

If pleasure and pain do not drive our behavior, what does? To find out, I conducted surveys of what people say motivates them. This led to the delineation of 16 basic desires that are deeply rooted in human nature and common to everyone.

CHAPTER 2

Research Identification of 16 Basic Desires

Four generations of Harvard University psychologists—William James (1842 – 1910), William McDougall (1871 – 1938), Henry Murray (1893 – 1988) and David McClelland (1917 – 1998)—suggested that psychological needs are the central organizing themes of behavior. James (1890/1950), who was influenced by Charles Darwin's (1859) theory of evolution of the species, suggested that human nature has a significant instinctual component. McDougall (2003/1908) held that human instincts play out in human behavior, culture, and religion. Murray (1938, 1943) renamed instincts as "psychological needs," suggesting they were influenced by the unconscious mind. David McClelland (1961) executed influential studies of achievement motivation and power. Further, Abraham Maslow (1954, 1943), who was at Brandeis University only a few miles from Harvard, published the influential idea of a "hierarchy" or "pyramid" of psychological needs.

McDougall (2003/1908) suggested the idea of a universal goal — meaning a goal that moves each of us. He wrote,

> Every man is so constituted to seek, to strive for, and to desire certain goals which are common to the species, and the attainment of which goals satisfies and allays the urge or craving or desire that moves us. These goals ... are not only common to all men, but also ... [to] their nearer relatives in the animal world; such goals as food; shelter from danger, the company of our fellows; intimacy with the opposite sex, triumph over our opponents, and leadership among our companions. [pp. 406-407]

McDougall viewed human nature as a group of distinct innate predispositions, which he regarded as the mainsprings to action. He called these predispositions "instincts" and suggested that they are essential for understanding social behavior, personality, and culture. McDougall suggested the following list of instincts:

- Flight from danger.
- Repulsion from pain.
- Curiosity in response to wonder about new places or things.
- Pugnacity when angered or threatened.
- Parenting (protecting and cherishing the young) when feeling tender emotions.
- Self-abasement (or subjection) when feeling negatively about oneself.
- Self-display (or dominance) when in the presence of spectators.

- Gregariousness (herd instinct) when lonely.
- Sex (reproduction) when aroused.

According to McDougall, the core of each instinct is an emotion. When we perceive danger, for example, we automatically (instinctively) experience fear, which motivates flight. Past learning might determine the place to which we flee, but the desire to flee from danger is instinctual. When we see a new place or thing, we automatically experience wonder, which motivates us to approach and examine the interesting place or object. How we study the new object — the way we manipulate or analyze it — might be learned, but the desire to approach new objects is deeply rooted in our nature.

McDougall's ideas raised almost as many questions as they were supposed to answer. What are the universal goals of mankind that motivate everyone? Is McDougall's list of principal instincts a valid taxonomy of universal goals? Is it comprehensive? How do universal goals impact personality, culture, and religion?

Many scholars objected to McDougall's concept of a human instinct. In his 1921 scholarly article "Giving Up Instincts in Psychology," Chinese psychologist Zing-Yang Kuo (1898 – 1970) argued that human beings have no complex behavior patterns that are innate or instinctual. Although McDougall responded to the criticisms, he didn't prevail. His use of the term "instinct" was too biological for psychologists to embrace and remains unpopular to this day. After McDougall published his work, psychologists suggested many alternative lists of universal goals and strivings, but the concept of a human instinct remained controversial.

Harvard professor Henry A. Murray (1943, 1938) suggested that universal motives are best understood as "psychological needs" rather than as "instincts." His aim was to integrate universal goals with psychoanalysis. He held that needs are partially determined by both infantile and early childhood experiences and by the unconscious mind. He recognized a biological basis to psychological needs but offered few details.

Murray considered "needs" as the organizing themes of our personality. Based on in-depth case studies, he initially identified the following 20 needs.

- Abasement, the need to surrender and accept punishment.
- Achievement, the need to overcome obstacles and succeed.
- Affiliation, the need for friendships.
- Aggression, the need to injure others.
- Autonomy, the need to resist others and stand strong.
- Counteraction, the need to defend honor.
- Defendance, the need to justify actions.
- Deference, the need to follow a superior.
- Dominance, the need to control and lead others.
- Exhibition, the need for attention.
- Harmavoidance, the need to avoid pain.
- Infavoidance, the need to avoid failure/shame or conceal weakness.
- Nurturance, the need to protect the helpless.
- Order, the need to arrange, organize, and be precise.
- Play, the need to relieve tension, have fun, or relax.
- Rejection, the need to exclude another.
- Sentience, the need for sensuality.
- Sex, the need for erotic relationships.
- Succorance, the need for support.
- Understanding, the need to analyze and know.

Murray acknowledged that his list "of needs is not very different from lists constructed by McDougall, Garnett, and a number of other writers." (Murray, 1938, p. 84). His work proved to be enormously influential for about 35 years.

In-depth studies of people relied on an assessment technique called the Thematic Apperception Test (TAT; Murray, 1943). Like the famous Rorschach inkblot assessment, the TAT is a "projective" method designed to assess unconscious psychodynamics. The examiner shows drawings of ambiguous scenes to the person whose needs are being assessed. For each of 20 drawings, the person is asked to make up a story with a beginning, a middle, and an end. The examiner interprets the stories by looking for common psychological themes. If several of the stories are about ambition, for example, the examiner might conclude that the individual has a strong need for achievement. First introduced in the 1936, the TAT became the primary method for evaluating an individual's psychological needs in clinical assessment.

In the 1960s and 1970s the TAT became increasingly controversial because of concerns about its subjectivity. Scientifically-minded psychologists had conducted hundreds of studies without producing convincing evidence for the validity of the results of the TAT. Some experts concluded that the stories people tell on the TAT reveal absolutely nothing about their psychological needs or personality.

When the scientific reputation of the TAT declined significantly, so did interest in the study of psychological needs. The TAT was vulnerable to a sharp decline in influence partially because of its limited practical implications. Its primary use was clinical diagnosis within a psychodynamic [Freudian] model. When the diagnostic model became obsolete, the TAT and Murray's psychological needs lost influence.

Douglas N. Jackson (1984) addressed the criticism that the TAT is "unscientific" by constructing a questionnaire that reliably and validly assessed Murray's needs. The questionnaire, called the Personality Research Form (PRF), did not have the impact it deserved, perhaps because it presumed the validity of Murray's taxonomy.

The influence of psychological needs theory declined in the 1965-1990 period with the rise of cognitive-behavior therapy. The cognitive-behavior therapists demanded that psychology be based on science and then attacked one sacred cow after another for lack of scientific support. Eysenck (1952), for example, questioned the scientific evidence for psychotherapy. Behaviorists also questioned the Freudian idea that early childhood experiences lead to adult strivings and personality needs (Ullmann & Krasner, 1965). Some behaviorists even questioned whether or not personality traits exist or could be scientifically proved.

The Harvard psychologists had suggested many lists of needs without scientifically validating any one of them.

Needs theory fared poorly when psychologists gave greater emphasis to scientific evidence. The Harvard psychologists had suggested many lists of needs without scientifically validating any one of them. McDougall's list of principal instincts was insightful and brilliantly reasoned, but his list did not meet scientific standards for reliability and validity, and he made no predictions that were scientifically evaluated. Absent a valid taxonomy of needs and a valid method to assess them, the influence of human needs theory declined to the point that it virtually disappeared from the academic journals.

By 1990, needs theory had become an oldie but goodie, a blast from the past, something nobody paid attention to except when studying history. Yet the basic insight is valid, namely, that there are certain goals (called "needs") that motivate everyone. In the words of behaviorists, some of whom say they don't like concepts like "needs," there are certain stimuli that reinforce everyone. Whether we call them instincts, needs, universal goals, intrinsic motives, or universal reinforcements, they are crucial for understanding how people behave in natural environments.

> *We embraced a new approach to the study of universal goals. If we want to identify these goals, why not ask people directly?*

THE 16 BASIC DESIRES

In the 1990s my colleagues and I set out to revive interest in needs theory. Specifically, we sought to address the three main reasons for its decline:

- absence of a scientifically valid taxonomy of needs;
- absence of a widely-accepted, scientifically valid assessment of the needs of any individual;
- few practical implications beyond clinical diagnosis within the outdated, DSM II framework.

We embraced a new approach to the study of universal goals. If we want to identify these goals, why not ask people directly? Why not design a questionnaire that would explore the life goals and fundamental values in people's lives? Perhaps that could yield a valid taxonomy of universal motives.

Surprisingly, no previous scholar had constructed a list of the universal goals of human nature by asking diverse groups of people what motivates them. Instead they suggested numerous lists of universal motives based on personal insights, observations of animals, anthropological studies, and in-depth case studies of the unconscious mind. The various lists were similar, but today none is considered to be scientifically valid.

I designed a questionnaire that basically asked people to tell us what goals matter to them. I began with a comprehensive list of motives based on suggestions from colleagues and friends. I consulted a variety of reference sources and solicited additional feedback from colleagues and graduate students. I collected more than 500 goals, but I pared the initial list to 328 by eliminating redundancies and candidates that seemed to have little psychological significance.

I knew that some psychologists take a dim view of questionnaires. People don't always know what they want, psychologists claim, and even when they do know, they may distrust researchers and not tell them. People are not always truthful. Some distort their responses out of embarrassment or defensiveness, while others seek to make themselves look good in the eyes of the researchers. (This latter group gives answers that are called "socially desirable" rather than valid.)

If you listen to enough research psychologists rattle off the shortcomings of questionnaires, you might come to the conclusion it's a waste of time to ask anybody anything. Yet in everyday life, asking leads to very valuable information. And so it can be in rigorous psychological research as well. Although it is reasonable to be concerned about distortion in questionnaire data, researchers can take well-established steps to reduce the risks.

I embraced a number of these methods to improve the validity of my results. Since participants completed the questionnaire anonymously, they knew the information they gave could not be used against them. They had no reason to withhold truthful responses.

We addressed the defensiveness issue in the way we phrased our questions. Psychologists have observed defensive reactions to questions like, "Are you bossy?" or "Are you sloppy?" We did not ask people about socially undesirable traits. We asked instead about their motives and values, as in "Do you enjoy leadership roles?" or "Do you want to be highly organized?" This gave people less reason to feel defensive or to distort their answers. ***On a questionnaire of what you want, you can get the results you want simply by answering in a straightforward and valid manner.***

Our first questionnaire study was a disaster. We asked people if they are motivated by sex, family, fear, and so on, and nearly everybody responded affirmatively to every question. Who doesn't enjoy sex, family, and eating? Who doesn't dislike anxiety and pain? I thought to myself: "No wonder nobody published this method before."

In an effort to turn a lemon into lemonade, I worked on rephrasing my questionnaire so it would yield useful results. Instead of inquiring whether people liked sex, I learned to ask, "Is sex essential to your happiness?" Everybody says they *like* sex, but only some people say that sex is "essential" to their happiness. Indeed, some of our research participants were so emphatic that sex is not "essential" to their happiness that our numerical rating scale of agreement/disagreement didn't cut it — they were moved to add comments such as "hell, no" in the margins.

We took advantage of our respondents' willingness to report the intensity of their desires. By rephrasing our questions as we did with, "Is sex essential," it became possible for us to measure individual variations in the strength of these universal goals. We may all share the same fundamental goals, but we invest them with varying degrees of intensity. Each of us cares about some of them more than others.

Having figured out how to ask fruitful questions, I now set out to construct a standard test of fundamental motives, or what is meaningful to us. With assistance from Susan Havercamp, at the time a graduate student, we executed five test development studies (Reiss & Havercamp, 1998). In each study we used a mathematical technique called factor analysis to identify goals that can be grouped together as manifestations of the same basic desire. Our 2,554 research participants ranged in age from 12 to 76 and included people with such diverse backgrounds as high school students, college students, soldiers, fast food workers, seminarians, human service providers, and nursing home residents, to give a few examples.

The results of our research identified 16 human needs. Throughout this book, I use the term "need" to refer to a group of related goals that motivate everybody. I use the term "basic desire" for the subjective experience of a need. For most purposes, I use the terms *need* and *basic desire* interchangeably.

Again, the 16 basic desires are as follows:

- Acceptance, the desire for positive self-regard.
- Curiosity, the desire for understanding.
- Eating, the desire for food.
- Family, the desire to raise children and spend time with siblings.
- Honor, the desire for upright character.
- Idealism, the desire for social justice.

- Independence, the desire for self-reliance.

- Order, the desire for structure.

- Physical Activity, the desire for muscle exercise.

- Power, the universal desire for influence or leadership.

- Romance, the desire for beauty and sex.

- Saving, the desire to collect.

- Social Contact, the desire for peer companionship.

- Status, the desire for respect based on social standing.

- Tranquility, the desire for safety.

- Vengeance, the desire to confront those who offend.

My colleagues and I have spent years accumulating scientific evidence that these 16 deeply rooted desires are intrinsic to all of us, and we have published articles and three books presenting our findings. By now we have assessed what motivates more than 60,000 people who come from all walks of life and from four continents (North America, Europe, Asia, and Australia). The studies on which we base our claims of scientific reliability and validity have been peer reviewed and have appeared in prestigious journals such as those published by the American Psychological Association.

What makes the list of 16 basic desires unique is its scientific status. We did not start by making up a list of basic desires and then setting out to validate our analysis. Instead, we empirically discovered the 16 basic desires based on what diverse groups of people from multiple countries and various continents told us about their own personal motives.

Each of the 16 basic desires is defined based on goals, aims, and intentions. Honor, for example, is a desire for character; independence is a desire for self-reliance; tranquility is a desire for safety; and vengeance is a desire to confront others and to win. I reject McDougall's idea that emotions are the essence of universal motives. Curiosity, for example, is temporarily satisfied by learning and understanding, not by the emotional joy of discovery. The need for romance is temporarily satisfied by sex, not by the emotion of ecstasy.

Why are basic desires defined by goals rather than emotions? I think goals are antecedents for future behavior, whereas emotions often are consequences of past or current behavior. Goals tell us what the individual wants and, thus, have implications for how the person is likely to behave in the future. Emotions tell us how the person feels and may or may not have implications for what the individual is likely to do in the future. If I know a young married person does not want to become a parent, I might predict that he or she would be compatible with a like-minded partner or would have repeated arguments with a partner who wants children. If I know that an individual is happily married and childless, I can't predict if he or she will have children in a year or two. People who plan to have children may be happy now without them, and people who plan to remain childless also may be happy now without them.

Basic desires are defined by goals, not emotions, because goals are more forward-looking and predictive of future behavior.

The 16 basic desires may have a genetic origin. They have been demonstrated for samples from four continents (North America, Europe, Asia, and Australia), and in multiple cultures. Further, a number of them can be observed for animals. Animals raise their young (indicating a desire for family), defend themselves (indicating a desire for vengeance), have sex (indicating a desire for romance), show fear (indicating a desire for tranquility), display dominance (indicating a desire for power), eat (indicating a desire for food), and exercise (indicating a desire for muscle exercise).

This is not to say that culture and upbringing play no role in determining the strength of the desires; certain desires may be encouraged in some cultures or families and suppressed in others. Two teachers, for example, might encourage their children to start reading at a very early age, while two athletes might encourage sports participation. Parents in a very small apartment might discourage uninhibited running around. Such differences in upbringing, especially in the early years, may strengthen or diminish the natural desires with which a child is born.

> *Since our basic desires have a genetic origin, we tend to have the same basic goals throughout our lives.*

Culture and upbringing also likely play significant roles in determining *how* people go about managing and gratifying their basic desires. People everywhere are motivated by hunger, power, curiosity, and so on, but they differ widely in the food they eat, how they go about satisfying their ambitions, and what they spend their time learning.

Since our basic desires have a genetic origin, we tend to have the same basic goals throughout our lives. People do not change much in what they fundamentally desire and intrinsically value. Curious children tend to become curious adolescents, who tend to become curious adults. People who have strong appetites tend to struggle with their weight all their lives. People who like to organize and plan things when they are adolescents probably will continue to enjoy organizing and planning when they are adults. I suspect that the underlying genes that influence these desires do not change much as we grow older.

(Although the basic desires usually change little throughout the adult years, people sometimes change how they satisfy them. A romantic person, for example, may change partners, a curious person may change topics of interest, or an athlete may change his or her preferred sports. Occasionally someone reports having changed their priorities after having found God. Nothing in my theory of 16 basic desires disputes such claims. I recognize the possibility that finding God or even experiencing the death of a loved one might change a person's priorities.

> *The 16 basic desires motivate our behavior, thoughts, images, and daydreams.*

The 16 basic desires motivate our behavior, thoughts, images, and daydreams. A person who is highly invested in the basic desire for family, for example, may think about family members when away on trips, look at pictures of their family when at work, and daydream about the next family vacation. People strongly motivated by the basic desire for power do more than pursue their career ambitions; they think about work during the evenings or on weekends, and they indulge in daydreams of becoming a CEO, great musician, or famous artist. Idealistic goals motivate some people to give generously to their favorite charities, to imagine a better society, and to work for political candidates they think may pass more just laws.

Perhaps the most important characteristic of a basic desire is its recurrent nature. These motives can be satisfied only temporarily, never permanently. We become hungry; we eat; and later we become hungry again. Everybody embraces the basic desire for eating, not for a day or two, not for a month or two, not even for a year or two. Eating is a recurrent basic desire for everyone from cradle to grave.

Similarly, all basic desires move us on and off, over and over, throughout the lifespan. We never permanently satisfy any of them. Each one recurs throughout our life on a frequent if not daily basis. The basic desire for curiosity, for example, has a recurrent nature: We become curious about something; we study and learn; and after a while we become curious about something else. The basic desire for social contact also has a recurrent nature: We are bored; we socialize for a while; we want to be alone for a spell; we become bored again and seek company.

> *Basic desires can be satisfied only temporarily, never permanently. They motivate us on and off, over and over, throughout the lifespan.*

In summary, we have reported the first ever research-derived taxonomy of universal motives and psychological needs. Our taxonomy of 16 needs has about 50 percent overlap with the lists of needs provided by McDougall, Murray, and others. We believe the 16 basic desires to have a genetic basis and a recurrent nature.

CHAPTER 3

Comprehensiveness of 16 Basic Desires

My colleagues and I believe that the list of 16 basic desires is comprehensive as is. We think it possible that some revisions will be needed with future study, but we consider it unlikely that major additions will be needed. We believe that all psychologically important motives express either one of the basic desires or two or more of them acting in compound. Sensuality, for example, is motivated by a compound of two basic desires: romance and eating.

This doesn't mean that our list is self-explanatory. Indeed, people ask many questions when they first see it. Like, "Isn't money a basic desire? Where's creativity? What about thirst?" Here is how we answer these questions.

First of all, we deliberately excluded some biological motives that have only minor psychological significance. Thirst, for example, has little relevance for understanding our personality, values, meaning of life, or culture. On the other hand, we included eating because of its cultural relevance, the time and effort people devote to preparing and consuming food, and its relevance to obesity and other medical concerns. Although many religions have dietary laws, few, if any, have laws governing how people should drink water.

The taxonomy of 16 basic desires is comprehensive. No psychologically important motive is left out.

Some critics have suggested that to exclude thirst adds a subjective element to our results. The fact of the matter is that many scientific classifications exclude the insignificant. Millions of rocks orbit the sun, but astronomers consider only eight of them to be significant enough to be classified as planets. Pluto was declassified from the list of planets because it is too small. In limiting the list of basic desires to *psychologically significant* motives — that is, motives relevant to personality, culture, or religion — we are operating within well-established scientific customs.

How does the desire to be wealthy fit into our schemata? What about people who embrace materialism by purchasing the most expensive homes, clothes, gadgets, and so on? Please recall that the 16 basic desires were defined by mathematical analysis of responses from thousands of people. Among those responses, we found a higher statistical congruity between the pursuit of wealth and the valuation of social status than between the pursuit of wealth and the valuations of power or security. Therefore, both materialism and wealth building are classified under the basic desire for status.

One reviewer of my previous book, <u>Who am I</u>, criticized me for treating beauty as part of the basic desire for romance. According to the reviewer, my idea that beauty and sex are linked perpetuates the stereotype of the highly sexed artist. I don't want to perpetuate stereotypes, but neither will I bow to political correctness. Beauty is a primal stimulus for sex: In every society since the first humans walked on Earth, people have wanted to appear beautiful to their partners prior to and during sex. If a desire for beauty were unconnected to the need for romance, as one of my critics has claimed, people would not care how they appeared to their partner prior to sex.

What about creativity? The desire to be original is not included in the list of 16 basic desires because it is not a universal goal shared by everyone. Many people do not aim to be original, and some do not even value it. Since creativity implies originality, it is not recognized as a basic desire. But creativity has another component — the desire to build or construct something. This goal falls under the basic desire for power, which is considered as a need for influence of will, or a need to make a difference. Similarly, the desire for achievement motivation falls under the basic desire for power.

Some evolutionary psychologists have wanted to know why survival is not among the 16 basic desires. The 16 desires include motives essential for survival such as eating, physical exercise, and cleanliness, but not a basic desire for survival itself.

I assume that in hunger the satiating goal is eating, not survival. I assume that when exercising the satiating goal is muscle activity, not survival. Survival is a common consequence of satisfying the basic desires for eating and physical activity, but it is not a common psychological goal.

In everyday life, survival per se motivates very little behavior. Except when I am very ill, I never think about trying to survive. Previous psychologists who studied human needs also did not include survival on their various lists. Widely-used psychological personality assessments do not assess traits for survivor. Evolutionary psychologist Douglas T. Kendrick at Arizona State University and I have discussed this issue on the *Psychology Today* website blogs, and he has argued that survival is not a basic desire as I define the term. Thus, I am in good company in not recognizing survival as one of the 16 basic desires of human nature.

What about the motives of attention, imitation, and play, which are so evident in children? McDougall thought that attention seeking is part of an instinctual self-display reaction to the presence of spectators, but I disagree. In adults, attention seeking is not a single motive but rather several motives depending on what it is we want others to notice. Seeking attention for wealth or social standing falls under the basic desire for status; seeking attention for achievement falls under the basic desire for power; and seeking attention for one's appearance falls under the basic desire for romance. Similarly, what motivates imitation depends on what it is we are imitating. Imitation of celebrities, for example, falls under the basic desire for status; imitation of achievers falls under the basic desire for power; while imitation of great lovers falls under the basic desire for romance.

Although some child psychologists have suggested that play is motivated by a desire for competence, adult play is more commonly about social interactions with peers. To understand adult play we need to look no further than the concept of a party. People play to have fun, and they play with others (rather than alone). In the taxonomy of the 16 basic desires, play and having fun fall under the basic desire for social contact.

Some psychologists have suggested that happiness is the most important basic desire. They are certainly right that it is human nature to want to be happy, but I think happiness is pursued indirectly and not as a principal end. To find happiness, you must aim to satisfy your strongest basic desires, and happiness will be experienced in passing.

Some religious people have criticized the 16 basic desires schema for not including a basic desire for God. I discuss this issue in Chapter 18. Briefly, I believe the concept of God addresses many human needs and, therefore, God is not a 17th basic desire unrelated to the other 16.

I hope these illustrations clarify what I was thinking when I established my taxonomy, which is not based on personal opinions or experience, but on statistical analysis of what many people told us. Like all scientific classification systems, the 16 basic desires are a work in progress and not an inalterable truth. Although we don't expect significant future changes, we are open to the possibility of modifications, provided they can be justified scientifically. *— see C. Jung*

If I had to suggest possible additions to my list of basic desires, territoriality would be my main candidate. In many species animals defend areas that contain a nest, mating site, and food for themselves and their young. They use scent markings — such as urination and defecation — to signal the boundaries of their territory. My dog, for example, defends the area where he usually sleeps. In humans territoriality is manifested by the maintenance of "personal space," defined as an area (usually only a few feet) surrounding the person. We feel discomfort, anger, or anxiety when our personal space is encroached without our permission. We allow into our personal space only people with whom we are familiar or intimate.

Humor is another possible candidate for inclusion in our list of basic desires. The case for including humor as a basic desire rests partially on the fact that people value it; it is relevant to our personality; and it is an important part of life. The case against including humor is that it isn't really a motive. Everyone enjoys humor, but many do not seek it out. Further, humor does not play out in religion, and it isn't a psychological dimension of meaningful experience. I suspect that humor does not have the necessary significance to be recognized as a basic desire, but it is a close call.

CHAPTER 4

Five Characteristics of a Basic Desire

Examination of the 16 basic desires reveals the following five common characteristics.

1. Universal Goals. The aim of each basic desire is a goal common to everyone and deeply rooted in human nature. The 16 universal goals are as follows:

- Avoidance of failure and rejection
- Understanding
- Food consumption
- Reproduction
- Character
- Justice
- Freedom

- Structure
- Muscle exercise
- Influence of will
- Sex
- Collections
- Belonging
- Respect
- Safety
- Revenge

2. Life Motives. Satiation of a basic desire is always temporary: Hours or days after a basic desire is temporarily satisfied, it somehow reasserts itself and influences behavior anew. When we eat, for example, it is only a matter of hours before we become hungry again. When we satisfy our curiosity about one topic, sooner or later we become curious about another topic.

> *Intrinsic motivation is the management of experience with universal goals in accordance with core values.*

Since basic desires can be satiated only temporarily, they motivate us from adolescence through adulthood. People show significant stability of motivation from adolescence through adulthood (Reiss & Havercamp, 2005).

3. Intrinsic Motivation. People pursue basic desires for no reason other than that is what they want. The basic desire for order, for example, motivates us to organize our lives because we intrinsically value structure, whereas the basic desire for acceptance motivates us to avoid criticism because we intrinsically value acceptance.

4. Core Values. Individuals vary significantly in how much value they place on each of the 16 basic desires. For example, athletes typically place significantly higher valuation on physical activity than does the average person. Intellectuals, on the other hand, typically place significantly higher valuation on understanding than does the average person.

Basic desires motivate everyone to express their core values. Again, basic desires (intrinsic motives) break down into two components: What is wanted (the universal goal), and how much is wanted (the individual's valuation of the universal goal). We do not seek infinite experience with each of the universal goals. Instead we seek to manage our experiences to express our values.

> *We are a species born to assert our core values.*

Intrinsic motives and core values are so closely connected we can infer core values from intrinsic motives, and we can infer intrinsic motives from core values. If you know that I am intrinsically motivated by family life, for example, you can infer that I value parenting and children. If you know that Peterson is intrinsically motivated by honor, you can infer that Peterson values character. Aristotle (1953/330 BCE) understood the close connection between values and motives. His book on motivation was titled <u>The Nichomachean Ethics</u>. For many years, moreover, philosophical inquiries on motivation were classified as ethical philosophy.

> *Intrinsic motives and core values are closely connected: We can infer core values from intrinsic motives, we can infer intrinsic motives from core values.*

5. *Psychological Significance*. A motive must have psychological significance to be considered a basic desire. This requirement permits us to ignore those universal motives that have no relevance for personality and relationships. Although our bodies are motivated to maintain a constant body temperature, I excluded homeostasis from my taxonomy of basic desires because it has nothing to do with psychology. Again, the exclusion of the insignificant is a well-established scientific method as exemplified in the de-listing of Pluto as a planet.

In conclusion, "basic desire" is the unit of analysis for determining what motivates somebody. By definition, a basic desire is the subjective component of a universal motive. The term is roughly equivalent to what others call "human need" or "intrinsic motive." Each basic desire has the five characteristics listed in this chapter. Again, the origin of basic desires is unknown. I assume they have a genetic component, although early childhood learning and possibly other experiences may affect them. We shouldn't let the seemingly endless nature-nurture debate prevent us from studying basic desires. We can use knowledge of basic desires to predict behavior in natural environments without knowing what causes those needs or where they come from.

> *We can use our knowledge of a person's needs to predict the individual's behavior in natural environments without knowing what caused those needs or from where they came.*

PART II

Motivation, Personality, and Relationships

CHAPTER 5

How Motives and Traits are Connected

Many psychologists who studied human needs spoke of "motivation and personality," but none provided a conceptual platform for connecting specific traits with specific needs. Maslow, for example, titled one of his books, <u>Motivation and Personality</u>, but he did not show how motives and traits are connected, as I attempt to do in this chapter.

To connect specific motives with specific traits, we need to consider each basic desire as a continuum of motivation. Table 5-1 provides some examples, and Figure 5-1 provides a conceptual diagram of the basic desire for social contact considered as a continuum of motivation.

Table 5-1. Basic Desires as Continua

Acceptance	How strong is the motivation to avoid failure and criticism?
Curiosity	How much time does the person want to spend thinking or analyzing?
Honor	How strictly does the individual obey a moral code of conduct?
Physical Activity	How much exercise does the person typically aim for?
Social Contact	How much time does the person want to spend with peers?

Figure 5-1. Basic Desire for Social Contact as a Continuum

Solitude   Social Experiences

0% Socializing _____100% Socializing

    ↑   ↑   ↑

Henry   Average Person Jake

As portrayed in Figure 5-1, each individual seeks to manage, regulate, and balance his/her experience toward a "satiation [set] point," which is also called an "optimal level of happiness," along each continuum. In Figure 5-1, the optimal level of happiness is indicated by an arrow (↑). Aristotle called these optimal levels of happiness, "golden means." They show what is "too much" (more than desired) versus "too little" (less than desired) experience with the universal goal.

As shown in Figure 5-1, the basic desire for social contact can be thought of as a continuum of motivation from wanting to be alone all of the time to wanting to socialize for all of one's waking hours. Each person has an optimal level of happiness for experiencing social contact. In Figure 5-1, for example, Henry is happiest socializing about 10% of his waking hours, while Jake is happiest socializing about 80% of the time. These numbers compare to the average person, or "norm," which for the sake of this example I assume to be 60% time socializing.

As shown in Figure 5-1, optimal levels of happiness vary for each individual. What is "too much" or "too little" social contact differs depending on individual. Each person has 16 optimal levels of happiness (16 satiation points), one for each basic desire.

Basic desires (intrinsic motives) have two aspects or qualities: **What** is wanted, and **how much** is wanted.

> *"I call a mean in relation to us that which is neither excessive nor deficient, and this is not one and the same for all."*
> —**(Aristotle, Book II, Nichomachean Ethics)**

- "What" is wanted is the universal in human motivation. We all want the same things: understanding, respect, sex, food, exercise, and so on.
- "How much" we want is the particular in human motivation. Although we all want understanding, for example, intellectuals value knowledge more than do non-intellectuals. Although we all want to exercise, active people want much more exercise than do inactive people.

A common error in psychological thought is to realize that everybody wants the same things without also recognizing the large individual differences in prioritization, valuation, and "how much." In a blog I posted at Huffington Post, I suggested that the way to motivate someone is to address his or her values.   One of the commentators to my blog did such a good job in clearly expressing the alternative view I have reproduced it below in order to respond to it.

> I dunno, Doc. I've spent my life motivating others. I find that everyone - from CEO's to street thugs - are motivated by a set of fairly consistent values. We all want respect. We all want to feel we all want love. The form each of those values takes may look different, but the values are pretty much universal.
>
> Of course, we're conflicted even about those values. While we yearn for safety and security, we also crave excitement and adventure. While we yearn to feel part of a community, we yearn for the personal power that comes from being unique and special.
>
> I've made a living motivating people. And received a lot of "you've changed my life" feedback over the years. But, I find that, in truth, I can't motivate anyone. People are motivated when they see someone living from a place of purpose and passion and joy -- and wake up to the fact that, whatever form those values take, that life lived with them is far happier and more satisfying than a life lived by default.

When it comes to motivating someone, the commentator argues that we do not have to appeal to individual values because everyone shares the same universal values. We can motivate people by appealing to these universal values. We all want respect, for example. We all want to belong.   Hence it should be possible to motivate others by appealing to their needs for respect and belonging.

The commentator makes an error I call the ***fallacy of the infinite***. Although we all want the same things, we want them to different extents. Everybody wants to be respected, but some people want much more respect than others, and they want it for different aspects of who they are. Everybody wants

> *Basic desires (intrinsic motives) have two aspects: **What** is wanted, and **how much** is wanted.*

to belong, but some need to belong much more strongly than do others.

The 16 desires show what everyone wants. The Reiss Motivation Profile®, a standardized psychological assessment, shows how individuals prioritize the 16 basic desires ("how much" they want). While everybody is motivated by social experiences such as belonging, introverts seek a much lower level of social experiences than do extroverts.

In order to connect basic desires and traits, we need to consider culture. In order to predict how Jake and Henry might behave based on Figure 5-1, for example, we need to compare "how much" social contact each desires with respect to the cultural norm. To understand how culture and motives combine to determine traits, let's analyze Figure 5-1 from Jake's vantage point: He wants social experiences 80% of the time, but just passing through his day without special effort to socialize provides 60% social time, much less than he wants. To experience an 80% social life, Jake needs to go out of his way to attract others to spend time with him. He might learn to be very friendly and likeable so people will want to spend extra time with him, or he might attend many parties. Since others will notice that Jake is more sociable than

> *Everybody wants the same things but not to the same degree.*

is the average person, he should gain a reputation for having a gregarious personality.

For Henry, passively going through his life provides much more social experience than he wants. He wants 10%, but his immediate culture provides 60%. Henry might become a grouch so others will not want to be with him. He might move to a remote area where nobody lives nearby. Since others will notice that Henry seems to avoid socializing, he might gain a reputation as a quiet person or perhaps an introvert.

Now let's analyze the situation for the average person. He or she wants about 60% social life, which is what the example assumes culture is deigned to provide to the typical person on an everyday basis. Individuals do not need to make much of an effort to satisfy an average desire for social life, so they show few distinctive behaviors that might gain them a reputation as a gregarious person or as a quiet person. Sometimes they are outgoing and take an interest in people, but at other times they want to be alone, so that their overall experiences balance to about 60% social contact.

> *Culture is designed to satiate normative desires, so that individuals with average needs can satisfy them without making special efforts.*

Everybody embraces all 16 basic desires, but individuals prioritize them differently. As the example of Henry and Jake suggests, high (significantly above average) and low (significantly below average) valuations of basic desires -- but not average valuations of basic desires -- produce personality traits. "High [need for] curiosity," for example, motivates an intellectual personality, whereas "low [need for] curiosity" motivates a practical personality. High independence motivates a proud personality, whereas low independence motivates a humble personality. High status motivates a formal personality ("stuffed shirt"), whereas low status motivates an informal personality.

The 16 basic desires make us individuals. Everybody embraces all 16, but individuals prioritize and value them differently. How we prioritize the 16 basic desires, called a Reiss Profile®, reveals our values and identifies what is meaningful to us. It is an expression of who we are.

Experience has taught us to provide case examples during the early phases of teaching people about the RMP and its underlying theory of 16 basic desires. Here I have chosen myself as your case example. I have done this because I know a lot about myself and because I know readers tend to be curious about the author when they read a book.

> *The 16 basic desires make us individuals.*

Please note that the case example is not evidence for the validity of the RMP or its underlying ideas. Obviously, what I say about myself is subject to all sorts of psychological distortions. The purpose of presenting the case example is to promote initial understanding of the theory of 16 basic desires and its application to understanding individuals. It isn't to provide evidence relevant to validity.

A summary of the results of my RMP is presented in Table 5-2. I have six "high" desires or "strong" needs, and I have five "low" desires" or "weak" needs.

Table 5-2. Author's RMP Results

High	Average	Low
Curiosity	Acceptance	Order
Eating	Family	Physical Activity
Idealism	Honor	Social Contact
Independence	Romance	Status
Power	Saving	
Vengeance	Tranquility	

Curiosity is the most outstanding motive in my life, and it has been this way since I was a child. I am always thinking about something, either a topic in psychology or something happening in my life. I read between two and four newspapers a day. I was in school for 57 uninterrupted years, first as a student and then as a professor. My curiosity did not end when I retired from academia: This is my third book written in retirement. In the last year or so, however, I have slowed down a bit in terms of how many hours I can do intellectual work on a typical day.

Since I am a curious person, ideas matter to me. When I think of who I am, I include specific ideas, such as "I am a person who thought of anxiety sensitivity." One of the first things people notice about me is that I make them think, and they react to me partially based on how much they enjoy intellectual activity.

Since I have a strong need for independence, I am sensitive to any limitation of my personal space. I resist anything that might limit my decision making, especially on personal or lifestyle matters. I want to do things my way because I value my individuality. I can be stubborn and difficult at times, not because I want to be stubborn or difficult, but rather because I cherish my individuality.

On the RMP power is about influence of will and motivates people to make a difference. It motivates me to work long hours. Many friends and colleagues think I work "too much," but they do not consider me to be a workaholic. I also satisfy my need for power by embracing leadership roles and by being assertive in my business affairs. Further, I have a competitive streak (which falls under a high score for vengeance) that motivates my interest in the business world and in sports.

Two RMP results -- high idealism and average honor -- mean I am more motivated to treat people fairly them I am to treat them in accordance with a specific code of ethics. Justice and fairness are very important to me; I am inclined to experience compassion for the needy. Whenever anybody suggests that I should do this or that -- "Steven, sign this contract, visit your friend in Chicago, give to this or that charity -- my first thoughts are, "Would the world be a better place if everybody so acted? Is it just? Is it fair?" Literally, that is what I automatically start to think.

To satisfy my high need for idealism, I devoted a significant part of my career to helping people with developmental disabilities and autism. Unlike many professionals in that field, I had no family interest. I was motivated by the knowledge I was helping people. I travelled widely training professionals to work with this population. I spoke in 44 U.S. states and a dozen countries. My humanitarian efforts were recognized with five national awards for research, leadership, and clinical services. I eventually decided to leave the field of disabilities to concentrate on my work on motivation. These ideas satisfy more of my needs, including curiosity (because of the effort at intellectual rigor), power (because of the opportunity for achievement), independence (because their uniqueness makes them mine), and idealism (because this work has significant implications for counseling or coaching people and for self-discovery).

Two RMP results -- high eating, low physical activity -- may explain why I have struggled with my weight most of my adult life. I am motivated to eat too much and to exercise too little.

In discovering who we are, weak basic desires are just as important as our strong ones. My RMP suggests that I place low valuation on four basic desires. I have a weak basic desire for status, which means that I am unimpressed with high society. I respect achievers -- great writers, athletes, business people -- but I am not impressed with status seekers. Further, I am an introvert or private person (which falls under a weak need for social contact).

Even the dullest observers of human nature notice that I am disorganized (which falls under a weak need for order). My office is a mess: My files are on the floor with papers falling out of them, and my wastebasket is overflowing with paper trash. I hate following schedules and have a tendency to arrive for appointments at the last second. I was at least 30 years old when I first bought an appointment book. Despite this major concession to organizing values, I continued to rush to appointments at the last minute just as I did before I used an appointment book. Although part of my schedule is now written in my appointment book, I often forget to look in the book.

In summary, my RMP shows how I prioritize 16 universal motives and reveals who I am in terms of personality, values, and what is meaningful to me. I am above all a 'Thinker," who has happily lived the life of an intellectual. My other outstanding traits are achiever, independent-minded, humanitarian, private, and disorganized. I intrinsically value ideas, achievement, personal freedom, fairness, and spontaneity.

CHAPTER 6

Traits Motivated by 16 Basic Desires

Wenow consider the conceptual platform I use to connect motives, traits, and values. There may be other conceptual platforms to accomplish this end, but I am unaware of them. The influential models of personality analysis — Freudian psychodynamics, the Big 5 personality theory, DSM (psychiatric) personality concepts — do not show how these aspects of human behavior are connected. We have assessed more than 60,000 people using this conceptual platform; the individuals we assessed agreed with the vast majority of the traits we suggested for them.

Aristotle noticed connections between traits and the valuation of a motive. According to Aristotle (1953/330 BCE, Book III), insufficient, moderate, and excessive degrees of the same basic desire can yield different, and even opposite, personality traits. For example, insufficient, moderate, and excessive predispositions to become fearful, respectively, are associated with the personality traits of foolhardiness, courage, and cowardice. Insufficient, moderate, and excessive desires for wealth, respectively, are associated with the personality traits of shabbiness, magnificence, and vulgarity.

Table 6-1 shows the theoretical connections between the 16 basic desires and personality traits. The table is intended to show how certain personality traits might be caused by the same motive but at different strengths of motivation. Here is how to read this table. *The need for acceptance is one of the 16 basic desires of humankind. Everybody is motivated to be accepted, but to different extents. People who have an insufficient (very weak) basic desire for acceptance appear to others as overconfident. Those with a low-intensity (or weak) basic desire for acceptance impress others as self-confident. People who have an average-intensity basic desire for acceptance make no distinctive impression on other people with regard to how confident they are. They may have confidence in some situations but lack confidence in others. People who have a high-intensity (or strong) basic desire for acceptance impress others as insecure and lacking in self-confidence. People who have an excessive (or very strong) basic desire for acceptance impress others as self-abasing.*

> *The same basic desire at varying degrees of strength produces different, even opposite, personality traits.*

Table 6-1. Personality Traits and Degree of Motivation

Basic Desire	Insufficient Motivation	Low Intensity Motivation	Average Motivation	High Intensity Motivation	Excessive Motivation
Acceptance	Overconfident	Self-confident	No trait	Insecure	Self-abasing
Curiosity	Mindless	Practical	No trait	Intellectual	Overly analytical
Eating	Malnourished	Thin	No trait	Overweight	Obese
Family	Childless	Absent parent	No trait	Responsible	Doting Parent
Honor	Unethical	Expedient	No trait	Trustworthy	Righteous
Idealism	Unjust, Unfair	Uninvolved	No trait	Humanitarian	True believer
Independence	Dependent	Interdependent	No trait	Self-reliant	Stubborn
Order	Chaotic	Disorganized	No trait	Organized	Perfectionist
Physical Activity	Inactive	Lazy	No trait	Energetic	Exhausting
Power	Submissive	Laid-back	No trait	Ambitious	Controlling
Romance	Abstinent	Undersexed	No trait	Romantic	Oversexed
Saving	Wasteful	Spender	No trait	Frugal	Miserly
Social Contact	Boorishness	Private	No trait	Friendly	Buffoonery
Status	Shabby	Informal	No trait	Formal	Snob
Tranquility	Fearless	Risk taker	No trait	Cautious	Coward
Vengeance	Conflict avoidant	Gentle, Kind	No trait	Warrior	Mean, Brutal

The remainder of Table 6-1 is read in a similar manner. Each of the 16 basic desires is a psychological need. Insufficient (very weak), low (weak), high (strong), and excessive (very strong) degrees of motivation produce the personality traits shown in the table. Average desires, however, create no distinctive impressions because the individual shows mixed traits from both the strong and weak categories.

The following comments show the theoretical connections between strong and weak basic desires, personality traits, and values. The order of presentation is alphabetical. These descriptions generally are backed by peer-reviewed scientific studies showing the validity of the RMP (see Chapter 20); many specific details, however, are still theoretical in nature and require future empirical evaluation. The system as a whole has been used professionally in counseling and coaching with more than 60,000 people; the feedback is uncommonly positive. All of the suggested connections between basic desires and personality traits are testable scientifically using the RMP standardized instrument.

ACCEPTANCE

Acceptance is the basic desire for positive self-regard. It motivates people to avoid criticism and rejection.

Satisfaction of this desire produces a feeling of self-confidence, whereas frustration produces feelings of insecurity.

Acceptance is the basic desire most relevant to self-esteem and self-concept. It motivates evaluation anxiety; that is, it is the reason people sometimes get nervous when they are evaluated or tested.

The overwhelming majority of people referred for psychological evaluation have a high need for acceptance. A low need for acceptance may indicate that the person is mentally healthy.

People with a **STRONG BASIC DESIRE FOR ACCEPTANCE** lack self-confidence. Typically they are insecure and have a tendency to be hurt by criticism, rejection, and failure. They see themselves in negative terms and are quick to blame themselves when something goes wrong. They may worry they will be judged inferior. Insecure people often require significant encouragement from others to try new things. Personality traits that may describe them include lacking self-confidence, downbeat, inconsistent effort, insecure, self-doubting, and perhaps indecisive or pessimistic.

People with a **WEAK BASIC DESIRE FOR ACCEPTANCE** are self-confident. Typically they have the basic optimism required to go after what they want in life and to expect success. They usually deal constructively with criticism, rejection, or failure. Personality traits that may describe them include confident, game (willing to try things), optimistic, and self-assured.

CURIOSITY

Curiosity is the basic desire for understanding.

Satisfaction of this desire produces a feeling of wonder, whereas frustration produces boredom or confusion.

Some experts confuse exploratory and intellectual curiosity. They claim that because babies explore their environments, everybody is born naturally curious. Young children start school so eager to learn they are wide eyed and thrilled. Rather than nurture this natural curiosity, say some experts, teachers unwittingly turn the fun of learning into a rat race for good grades and academic awards. In no time at all, schools extinguish the natural curiosity of their students. The students now hate school and lack motivation.

This myth is right on two counts: Babies enjoy exploring their environments, and many middle and high school students dislike school. The error is in assuming that the exploratory behavior of babies has something to do with the intellectual behavior of adolescents. I am not sure that it does.

The theory of 16 basic desires distinguishes between the need for cognition, which falls under the basic desire for curiosity, and the desire to explore one's environment, which as adventure falls under the basic desire for tranquility. Consider the people you know who are explorers. Notice that only some of them are also thinkers. Now consider the people you know who are thinkers. Notice that only some of them are also explorers. Although some social psychologists have assumed that exploring (e.g., babies roaming environments) and thinking (e.g., students learning math) are commonly motivated by a need for stimulus novelty, the fact that thinkers aren't necessarily explorers and vice versa suggests otherwise.

Daniel Boone was a legendary eighteenth century explorer who has been described by his biographer, John Filson (2010), as a "curious" man because Boone loved to explore new places. Yet Boone also hated school and, thus, probably had a low need for intellectual understanding. In contrast, Issac Newton was among the most influential intellectuals ever. He had a thirst for knowledge even as a young boy. Although Newton was always thinking, he wasn't much for exploring. He spent many months more or less alone in his Cambridge University dormitory working on exciting new mathematical ideas.

Explorers like Boone aren't necessarily intellectuals like Newton, and intellectuals like Newton aren't necessarily explorers like Boone. We should not assume that exploratory and intellectual behavior is motivated by a common curiosity.

Instead the theory of 16 basic desires recognizes two kinds of curiosity, called exploratory and intellectual. Exploratory curiosity is the result of attraction of novel stimuli, while intellectual curiosity is about ideas and the need for cognition. The exploratory behavior of babies does not imply that high school students were born with a natural curiosity for intellectual learning.

\ Although exploratory and intellectual curiosities are two different motives, coincidentally some people enjoy both exploring and thinking. John Glenn, the first man to walk on the moon, enjoyed science. Edmund Hillary, the first man to explore the peak of Mount Everest, wrote a number of books. The mythical men of the starship Enterprise were scientists: Known throughout the universe as a great thinker, Spock boldly went where no man had gone before.

In conclusion, the basic desire for curiosity is about intellectual understanding and does not including exploring, which falls under weak basic desires for acceptance and tranquility.

People with a **<u>STRONG BASIC DESIRE FOR CURIOSITY</u>** embrace intellectual pursuits such as thinking, reading, writing, and conversing. Their ideas and theories mean a great deal to them. They show a wide range of intellectual interests even though they may focus on a particular area of expertise. Personality traits that may describe them include contemplative, deep thinker, inquisitive, intellectual, reflective, and thoughtful.

People with a **<u>WEAK BASIC DESIRE FOR CURIOSITY</u>** like to keep their intellectual activity to a minimum. They become easily frustrated when they try to think. They rarely read books, debate ideas, or enjoy intellectual conversations. They may have little patience with intellectual matters and even may view intellectuals in a negative light. They may like to speak with actions rather than words. As former football great Johnny Unitas put it, "Talk is cheap – let's do our talking on the field." Personality traits that may describe them include action-oriented, nonintellectual, and practical.

EATING

Eating is the basic desire for food.

Satisfaction of this desire produces feelings of satiation or fullness, whereas frustration produces feelings of hunger.

Since eating is essential for life, many psychologists believe it is an especially strong desire. Abraham Maslow (1954) wrote that eating takes primacy over psychological motives, as in the example of hunger pains interrupting someone who is reading a book. Maslow believed that hunger and other biological survival needs must be gratified before other basic needs can motivate us.

People with a **<u>STRONG BASIC DESIRE FOR EATING</u>** have hearty appetites. They may enjoy many different kinds of food. In adulthood they may become overweight. Personality traits that may describe them include gluttonous, overeater, voracious, and possibly hedonistic.

People with a **<u>WEAK BASIC DESIRE FOR EATING</u>** have little appetite for food. They may be fussy about what they eat. Personality traits that may describe them include eats like a bird, eats sparingly, fussy eater, light eater, and possibly thin.

FAMILY

Family is the basic desire to raise one's children and to spend time with siblings. It encompasses what is commonly called the maternal and paternal instincts.

Satisfaction of this desire produces feelings of parental love, tenderness, and feeling needed. Frustration of this desire produces feelings of unhappiness. This desire, which binds parent to child, is unrelated to the basic desire for honor, which binds child to parent.

This desire motivates people to value their family – including children, brothers, and sisters – and to be attentive to their family's needs. It may prod people to support education, coach Little League, or serve as a Boy/Girl Scout leader.

People with a **STRONG BASIC DESIRE FOR FAMILY** want to have children and spend significant time raising them. Their children may be everything to them. Personality traits that may describe them include family person, family values, loving person, motherly (or fatherly), and perhaps nurturing.

People with a **WEAK BASIC DESIRE FOR FAMILY** consider the duties of parenthood to be burdensome. They may not want to become a parent. If they have children, they may not spend much time raising them. Personality traits that may describe them are wants to be childless, noninvolved parent, and absentee parent.

Honor

Honor is the basic desire for upright character. It motivates people to embrace moral codes of conduct.

Satisfaction of this desire produces feelings of loyalty, whereas frustration produces feelings of guilt and shame.

Honor motivates loyalty to one's parents and clan. It motivates pride in ethnic heritage. By embracing the moral code of our parents, we honor them. We also honor our parents by embracing their religious denomination and making it our own.

People with a **STRONG BASIC DESIRE FOR HONOR** are righteous. They may be focused on issues of character, morality, and principle. They may be loyal to their ethnic group and parents. Personality traits that may describe them include dependable, genuine, honest, loyal, principled, sanctimonious, scrupulous, sincere, steadfast, trustworthy, truthful, and upright.

People with a **WEAK BASIC DESIRE FOR HONOR** are expedient. They are inclined to do whatever it takes to get an important job done. Personality traits that describe them include expedient and opportunistic.

Idealism

Idealism is the basic desire for social justice. It motivates people to support social causes, pay attention to current affairs, or give to charities.

Satisfaction of this desire produces feelings of compassion, whereas frustration produces feelings of outrage.

According to the theory of 16 basic desires, conscientiousness breaks down into honor and idealism. Honor binds us to our clan or ethnic group, while idealism binds us to humanity as a whole. These two aspects of conscientiousness are only moderately correlated with each other and, thus, need to be assessed separately.

People with a **STRONG BASIC DESIRE FOR IDEALISM** may care deeply about such social causes as world peace, uplifting the downtrodden, or world health. Personality traits that may apply to them include altruistic, compassionate, do-gooder, dreamer, fair, humanitarian, idealistic, involved, volunteer, philanthropic, and perhaps martyr.

People with a **WEAK BASIC DESIRE FOR IDEALISM** are focused on the events in their lives rather than on the great issues facing society. They may think that injustice is part of life and there is little one should do about it unless it directly affects oneself or loved ones. Personality traits that may apply to them include hard-nosed, pragmatic, man (woman) of the world, realistic, and possibly looks the other way.

INDEPENDENCE

Independence is the basic desire for self-reliance. It motivates people to make their own decisions and to value their personal freedom.

Satisfaction of this desire produces the joy of personal freedom, whereas frustration produces feelings of dependency.

Independence motivates how much we want to stand out as individuals. It is especially strong during adolescence. Many teenagers who are strongly motivated by independence find ways to call attention to their individuality, such as wearing unusual clothes.

People with a **STRONG BASIC DESIRE FOR INDEPENDENCE** are self-reliant. Their personal freedom may be everything to them; they may dislike being in need of others. It may be very important to them that things be done their way ("my way, or the highway"). They may not "go along, to get along." They may feel uncomfortable being intimate. Personality traits that may describe them include autonomous, independent, self-reliant, and perhaps proud, stubborn, and uncomfortable with touchy-feely experiences.

People with a **<u>WEAK BASIC DESIRE FOR INDEPENDENCE</u>** trust others to meet their needs. They value psychological support, especially when making decisions. They may devalue displays of individuality. They may seek mystical experiences such as "unity of consciousness," nirvana, "being in the zone," "peak experience," and "flow." Personality traits that may describe them include humble, interdependent, and perhaps mystic or likes touchy-feely experiences.

ORDER

Order is the basic desire for structure. It motivates people to plan, schedule, and organize.

Satisfaction of this desire produces a sense of comfort, whereas frustration produces feelings of discomfort.

People with a **<u>STRONG BASIC DESIRE FOR ORDER</u>** are organized. Tidiness and punctuality are very important to them. Typically, they pay attention to details, rules, and schedules, and they may be comfortable with predictable and relatively unchanging situations. They tend to embrace rituals. Personality traits that may describe them include careful, inflexible, methodical, neat, organized, orderly, precise, prepared, punctual, thorough, and tidy.

People with a **WEAK BASIC DESIRE FOR ORDER** are flexible. They may have a high tolerance for ambiguity. Typically, they dislike structure and hate following rules and schedules. They often change their mind or their plans. They focus on the "big picture" to the extent of perhaps missing key details. Personality traits that may describe them include disorganized, flexible, follows nose, hates planning, keeps options open as long as possible, spontaneous, tardy, and untidy.

PHYSICAL ACTIVITY

Physical activity is the basic desire for muscle exercise. This desire motivates people toward physically vigorous activity, such as sports.

Satisfaction of this desire produces the joy of vitality, whereas frustration produces restlessness.

According to the results of the RMP with various college athletic teams (Reiss, Wiltz, & Sherman, 2001), five motivational traits define the "Athletic Personality": strong basic desires for physical activity, family, power (achievement), vengeance (competition), and social contact. The most important motive, of course, is a very strong basic desire for physical activity.

People with a **STRONG BASIC DESIRE FOR PHYSICAL AC-TIVITY** seek an active lifestyle. Workouts or sports are an important part of their lives. They may value fitness, vitality, strength, and stamina. Personality traits that may apply to them are active, athletic, energetic, fit, outdoorsy, perky, and physical.

People with a **WEAK BASIC DESIRE FOR PHYSICAL ACTIV-ITY** prefer a sedentary lifestyle. They need encouragement and extrinsic reasons – such as health – to exercise regularly. Personality traits that may apply to them are lackadaisical, listless, inactive, lethargic, and sedentary lifestyle.

POWER

Power is the basic desire for influence or leadership. It motivates willpower, the need for achievement, and hard work. It motivates us to seek to influence people, events, or the environment. Power motivates the desire to lead and to give advice. It has been said of some powerful personalities that they cannot stand to see somebody go in one direction without urging the person to go in a different direction.

Satisfaction of this desire produces the joy of self-efficacy and feelings of competence, whereas frustration produces regret, or possibly feelings of inferiority or humiliation.

The primal association between achievement and power is apparent at athletic contests. When a team scores a goal, for example, the fans thrust clenched fists into the air in a display of power.

I tentatively classify the desire to build things as an influence of will. According to James (1890/1918) and McDougall (1908/2003), the need for construction is as genuine and irresistible an instinct in man as it is in the bee and beaver. The satisfaction of building something is very real, quite apart from the value or usefulness of the object made.

Please notice that winning and achievement fall under different basic desires. The need to win is motivated by the basic desire for vengeance, whereas the need to achieve is motivated by the basic desire for power. Writing a book and building a house, for example, are achievements motivated by power but not vengeance.

People with a **STRONG BASIC DESIRE FOR POWER** like to take charge of situations and assume leadership roles. They may seek out challenges and work hard to accomplish their goals. They may enjoy giving others advice. Personality traits that may describe them include ambitious, assertive, bold, hardworking, determined, domineering, focused, single-minded, and willful.

People with a **WEAK BASIC DESIRE FOR POWER** dislike self-assertion. They tend to let events unfold without trying to influence them. They may be nondirective and lacking in ambition. They may dislike leadership roles and may dislike giving advice or guidance to others. They may keep their work and career in perspective by giving at least equal weight to personal and family life. They may avoid achievement goals that are challenging. They are not lazy or unconcerned; they are motivated instead by an intrinsic dislike of controlling and influencing others. Personality traits that may describe them include easygoing, laid-back, onlookers, nonassertive, nondirective, and unambitious.

ROMANCE

Romance is the basic desire for beauty and sex. It motivates people to care about their appearance and to pursue potential sex partners. The striving for romance is moderately correlated with the desire to experience beauty.

Satisfaction of this desire produces feelings of ecstasy, whereas frustration produces feelings of lust.

Romance is not part of a larger desire for sensual pleasure. The goal of romance is sex, not sensual pleasure; the goal of eating is food, not sensual pleasure. If human beings were motivated by sensual pleasure rather than by separate and unrelated desires for romance and eating, it would be possible to satiate hunger by having sex. Sensual pleasure is a signal that you have experienced your goal; it is not the goal itself.

People with a **STRONG BASIC DESIRE FOR ROMANCE** seek active sex lives. They may value sexual skills or passion. They often may think about sex. They may be attracted to many potential partners. Personality traits that may apply to them are amorous, flirtatious, lover, oversexed, passionate, romantic, and perhaps promiscuous.

People with a **WEAK BASIC DESIRE FOR ROMANCE** may spend little time thinking about, and pursuing, sex. Personality traits that may apply to them include ascetic, celibate, chaste, Platonic, puritanical, and undersexed.

SAVING

Saving is the basic desire to collect things. People collect many different objects including antiques, art, autographs, automobiles, books, clothes, coins, firearms, furniture, jewelry, magazines, military memorabilia, music, photographs, religious relics, sports memorabilia, stamps, tools, and toys.

Satisfaction of this desire produces the pride of ownership, while frustration produces worrying about being unprepared.

This basic desire is correlated to the tendency to save or spend money, but it does not measure this tendency directly.

People with a **STRONG BASIC DESIRE FOR SAVING** are collectors. They may hate throwing things away and may be tight with money.

Personality traits that may describe them include saver, accumulator, collector, hoarder, pack rat, and possibly frugal and thrifty.

People with a **WEAK BASIC DESIRE FOR SAVING** tend to use things and then dispose of them. Personality traits that may describe them include spendthrift, profligate, wasteful, and possibly extravagant.

SOCIAL CONTACT

Social contact is the basic desire for companionship with peers.

Satisfaction of this desire produces feelings of fun and belonging, whereas frustration produces feelings of loneliness.

William McDougall (1908/2003) suggested that human beings are born with a "gregarious instinct," or an inborn tendency to live in small groups such as herds or tribes. This basic desire creates a psychological need for friends. People who want many friends learn social graces and skills to attract and keep them. The desire to socialize is so highly valued that withholding opportunities to socialize – as in ostracism – is a form of punishment.

This basic desire is about companionship with peers and does not include companionship with parents and children. How much time a person wants to spend with his or her parents or children does not predict how much time the individual wants to spend with peers. The strivings for honor and family, respectively, motivate interest in parents and children. Further, the basic desire for social contact is not satisfied by time spent with lovers, which falls under the basic desire for romance. Only the striving for social contact motivates interest in peers.

People with a **STRONG BASIC DESIRE FOR SOCIAL CONTACT** are friendly. They may show mannerisms and habits that attract others. They may be fun loving and upbeat. Personality traits that may describe them include affable, charming, cheerful, engaging, extroverted, friendly, fun-loving, gracious, gregarious, outgoing, playful, prankster, sociable, vivacious, and warm.

People with a **WEAK BASIC DESIRE FOR SOCIAL CONTACT** enjoy solitude. They dislike parties, small talk, and socializing, and they may show little interest in most people they meet. They may have few friends. They often seem to be in a serious mood. Personality traits that may describe them include quiet, private, serious, introvert, aloof, brusque, detached, distant, and possibly withdrawn.

STATUS

Status is the basic desire for respect based on social standing. Although psychoanalyst Alfred Adler (1971/1929) suggested that people seek status to compensate for unconscious feelings of inferiority, the theory of 16 basic desires assumes that people seek status because they intrinsically value self-importance and respect.

Satisfaction of this desire produces feelings of superiority, whereas frustration produces feelings of inferiority.

Generally, the attention other people pay us is a primal indicator of our status. People pay attention to important people and ignore unimportant people.

Your status is an indicator of how much respect and deference is your due. People feel slighted when they receive less deference than is their due, and they feel flattered when they receive more deference than is their due. Status motivates people to pay attention to and value their reputation.

Status motivates materialistic values including living in prestigious residential neighborhoods, owning expensive cars, and wearing designer clothes.

Status motivates people to consider social class when choosing a potential spouse. People with a strong desire for status may aim to marry up in class – that is, marry someone who is wealthy, or marry someone who is beautiful or handsome (a so-called "trophy" spouse). People with a weak desire for status, however, may disregard money or social class when choosing a spouse.

Status motivates interest in clothes. "White-collar" workers, for example, have higher status than do "blue-collar" workers. Lawyers dress in three-piece suits to project the image of success; physicians dress in lab coats to project an image of scientific expertise; and priests dress plainly to show their status before God.

The basic desires for status and power are correlated, perhaps because of a common origin. Unlike animals, human beings can gain dominance in two ways: merit versus inheritance. People can have high status as a consequence of great achievement or as a consequence of high birth. Some people feel important because of their achievements (which falls under the basic desire for power), whereas others feel important because of their high birth, wealth, good looks, or fame (which falls under the basic desire for status). Achievers look down on royals as undeserving of great respect, whereas royals look down on achievers because they needed to work to become important. Royals pride themselves in their idleness precisely to make the point that they are so important they do not have to work.

People with a **<u>STRONG BASIC DESIRE FOR STATUS</u>** value wealth, material things, and social class. They may associate themselves with anything that is popular and may dissociate themselves from anything that is unpopular. They may admire high society and may be impressed with marks of social distinction such as titles and privileges. They may be motivated to embrace the mannerisms, dress, and habits of prestigious or wealthy people. They may like to be associated with the "right" people, and they may be impressed by membership in prestigious social clubs. Personality traits that may apply to them are formal, materialistic, patrician, proud, lofty, and dignified.

People with a **WEAK BASIC DESIRE FOR STATUS** are unimpressed with high society, wealth, and fame. They believe it is wrong to admire someone just because he/she happened to be born into a certain family or is wealthy. They may not care what others think of them. They may identify with the middle or lower class. Personality traits that describe them are casual, down-to-earth, egalitarian, informal, and unceremonious.

TRANQUILITY

Tranquility is the basic desire for safety. It has survival benefits because it motivates avoidance of danger. Danger is diabolical – it threatens yet excites us. We seek a balance between safety and excitement. This desire influences attitudes toward danger, adventure, and to a lesser extent, possibly financial risk.

Satisfaction of this desire produces feelings of relaxation, whereas frustration produces fear, anxiety, worry, or pain.

People with a **STRONG BASIC DESIRE FOR TRANQUILITY** place a high value on their personal safety. They may have many fears and may be highly sensitive to physical pain. They may worry about money, romance, job, health, or the future (Horney, 1939). They may be risk avoidant. Personality traits that describe them include fearful, anxious, cautious, timid, and possibly worrier.

People with a **WEAK BASIC DESIRE FOR TRANQUILITY** may be fearless. They may have a high capacity for handling stress. They may expose themselves to danger. Personality traits that may describe them are brave, calm, courageous, explorer, fearless, risk-taker, relaxed, and adventurous.

VENGEANCE

Vengeance is the basic desire to confront those who offend.

Satisfaction of this desire produces the joy of vindication, whereas frustration stimulates the fighting spirit and possibly anger.

The desire for vengeance motivates the competitive spirit. Competitive people are not necessarily physically aggressive, but they are quick to confront others. Competitive people value winning.

The primal provocations are threats to your status, your territory, and your children; competition for resources; access to potential mates; strange or unfamiliar people; and aggressive or unfriendly displays by other people (see Aureli & de Waal, 2000).

We have the potential to use peacekeeping and reconciliation behavior to manage aggressive impulses. These behaviors include submissive displays, sharing, cooperative play, apologies, holding hands, and kissing. Reconciliation behavior signals the end of a conflict and serves to reduce future conflict (see Aureli & de Waal, 2000).

The inclination toward aggressiveness is stable over much of the lifespan. Relative to the people your age, you are predicted to be about as aggressive 10 or 20 years from now as you are in the current phase of your life. Researchers have shown, for example, that disproportionate numbers of schoolyard bullies grow up to become criminals.

People with a **STRONG BASIC DESIRE FOR VENGEANCE** are quick to confront others. They value competitors and winners. Personality traits that may describe them include competitor, fighter, pugnacious, and perhaps aggressive, angry, argumentative, combative or mean.

People with a **WEAK BASIC DESIRE FOR VENGEANCE** avoid confrontation, fights, and violence. Often their first impulse is to cooperate rather than to compete. They may search for ways to settle problems amicably. Personality traits that may apply to them include cooperative, kind, merciful, non-aggressive, and peacemaker.

CHAPTER 7

Why Maslow's Hierarchy is Invalid

Figure 7-1. Maslow's Needs Hierarchy

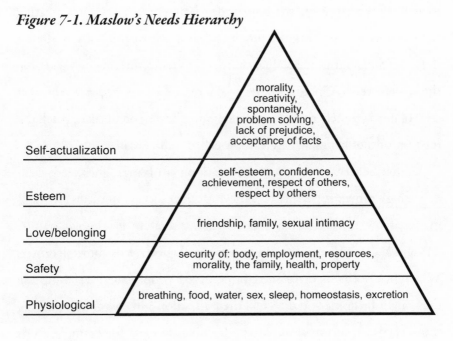

Self-actualization — morality, creativity, spontaneity, problem solving, lack of prejudice, acceptance of facts

Esteem — self-esteem, confidence, achievement, respect of others, respect by others

Love/belonging — friendship, family, sexual intimacy

Safety — security of: body, employment, resources, morality, the family, health, property

Physiological — breathing, food, water, sex, sleep, homeostasis, excretion

The RMP is intended to replace what Abraham Maslow (1943) called the "pyramid of needs," which is shown in Figure 7-1. I sometimes compare my theory to Maslow's in order to sharpen exactly what I assert in my theory of 16 basic desires. Maslow's theory peaked in influence during the 1960s, when he was president of the American Psychological Association, but it remains influential today, especially among human resource managers.

> *The scientific researchers who evaluated Maslow's theory discovered that it has little validity.*

Maslow's theory is based on two ideas. First, he recognized five categories of human needs, or what I call basic desires. These are needs of the body, safety needs, belonging needs, esteem needs, and what he called self-actualization. Second, he embraced the idea of adult human development. According to his theory, everybody starts the human development process concentrating their efforts at mastering the physiological needs of the body, and after they accomplish this, individuals move on to concentrating on mastering their safety needs. Once this latter goal is reached, we move on to the next level of needs, which are lover and belonging, and so on until we reach the highest form of being, which Maslow called "self-actualization".

Maslow held that we do not concentrate on satisfying higher needs, such as finding a romantic partner or achieving career success, until after we have mastered lower needs such as food, shelter, and safety. It is human nature, he suggested, to give priority to unmet physiological needs above all others. When such needs are unsatisfied, he observed, people stop everything else they might be doing and direct all their attention and energy to satisfying those needs. A person at work who becomes hungry, for example, stops work in order to eat. A child who feels cold stops playing and goes inside to dress warmly. Observations such as these convinced Maslow that people satisfy physiological needs before they gratify any other kind of need.

When the individual masters physiological needs, the person moves on to concentrate on satisfying safety needs. The physiological needs, now mastered, are pushed into the background, and safety becomes the individual's most important concern. When these needs are mastered, the individual, now relaxed and non-anxious, moves on to joining organizations and to having a successful career. Mastery of these needs leads to feelings of self-confidence, worth, and capability, but people have feelings of inferiority and helplessness when these needs are thwarted.

If all the needs discussed thus far are mastered, Maslow believed a new restlessness sometimes occurs. It is the need for self-fulfillment, to become everything that one is capable of becoming. It is at this stage that our individuality is most fully developed. A musician must make music, an artist must paint, and a poet must write.

Maslow's pyramid is similar to Hindu scripture, specifically the Rig Veda, which refers to the chakras. This is a seven level energy system that maps to specific psychological characteristics. They are as follows:

- 1st Chakra–Muladhara (Root, located at the perineum), motivates the survival instinct.
- 2nd Chakra–Swadhisthana (Sacral, located in the lower abdomen, just below the navel), motivates sexual passion.
- 3rd Chakra–Manipura (Solar Plexus), motivates self-power or will.
- 4th Chakra–Anahata (Heart), motivates love.
- 5th Chakra–Vishuddha (Throat), motivates learning and independence.

- 6th Chakra–Ajna (Brow or Third Eye), motivates self-awareness and insight.
- 7th Chakra–Sahasrara (Crown, located in the center of the skull, opposite the Root), motivates self-actualization.

Although it is not widely known, Maslow may have borrowed four ideas from Hinduism:

- pyramid of needs;
- progression through different developmental stages during which specific needs are dominant;
- first stage of human development is about survival needs;
- last stage of human development is about self-actualization.

The scientific researchers who evaluated Maslow's theory discovered it has little validity. Even researchers who started out sympathetic to Maslow's ideas eventually concluded that his pyramid of needs is invalid. By about 1975, the research community had more or less reached a negative consensus. I am unaware of any influential scientists who claim the pyramid is valid.

One problem with Maslow's pyramid is that human needs do not divide into its five categories. As shown in Table 7-1, Maslow's categories lump together unrelated basic desires. In Maslow's pyramid, for example, the need for family is about safety, but according to the results of research on the 16 basic desires, the need for family is about children. Maslow has honor as a lower need and idealism as the highest need, but this speculative classification of needs is invalid. The scientific research on both the 16 basic desires and the Big 5 concept of conscientiousness shows that honor and idealism are correlated motives and, thus, couldn't be at different stages of development as Maslow surmised. Although Maslow's idea that raising a family satisfies social needs may seem valid, it isn't. Family is about parenting, whereas social contact is about playing with peers. Families don't party, and partygoers aren't necessarily parents. Family and social contact are different needs of human nature.

Table 7-1. Maslow's Needs and Basic Desires

Maslow's Needs	Basic Desires
Physiological Needs	Eating, Physical Activity, Romance
Safety	Tranquility, Order, Honor, Family, Saving, Vengeance
Belonging, Love	Social Contact, Independence
Esteem	Acceptance, Power, Status
Self-Actualization	Idealism, Curiosity

Another problem with Maslow's pyramid of needs is that it underestimates individuality. Whereas Maslow assumed a universal pyramid of needs applicable for everyone, our research on the 16 basic desires shows that each individual has a unique pyramid of needs. Everybody has a personal pyramid that shows what is meaningful to him or her. Maslow's concept of a universal pyramid is invalid.

People do not undergo a process of satisfying one set of needs and then moving on to another, as Maslow claimed. By adolescence most people have prioritized the 16 basic desires in ways that will endure for the rest of their lives. Athletic adolescents become physically active adults; they do not move on from being active people to become somebody else. Friendly adolescents become gregarious adults; disorganized adolescents become disorganized adults; and so on.

> *People are more or less motivated by the same basic desires throughout their adult life. Maslow's idea of human development — that values and motives change as we mature — is mostly an invalid, romantic myth.*

Reiss and Havercamp (2005) tested Maslow's theory by looking at how the strength of the 16 basic desires varies with age. We divided 1,712 respondents into four age groups, and we looked at the sum of all 16 basic desires, which we called "total motivation," as well as each desire individually. Our results showed the following:

Total motivation increased during adolescence and young adulthood. The young people were passionate about many things.

- Total motivation peaked during middle age. Middle-aged adults neither gained nor lost passion.
- Total motivation fell for seniors, and the rate of decline accelerated with advancing age. Elderly people cared less than young people about almost everything except the basic desire for tranquility, which became higher in the later years of life.

We found little evidence for Maslow's five stages of human development. People were not concentrating on, say, safety needs during one part of their lives and then moving on to belonging needs. With advancing age the desires declined.

As was discussed earlier, I have been an intellectually curious person since adolescence. I spend much of my time thinking, analyzing, reading, writing, and engaged in intellectual conversations. I have been this way since high school, when I spent the summer before my senior year taking a college course in philosophy because I enjoyed it. The idea that I underwent a human development process in which my intellectual curiosity emerged at some later date after I had first mastered physiological, safety, and belonging needs is simply not true. Although we might change and grow as we mature, we do not change in anywhere near the dramatic fashion implied by Maslow's imaginative pyramid. We do not go from one set of needs to the next, which would imply changing from one set of personality traits to another.

In conclusion, every person has his or her own pyramid of needs. The RMP assesses an individual's unique pyramid of needs. Your needs reveal who you are, not how you measure up against some universal standard of humanity represented in Maslow's Pyramid.

CHAPTER 8

How Needs Play Out in Relationships

The theory of 16 basic desires has significant implications for relationships. By assessing the motives and values of any two people — romantic partners, parent-child, executive-underling — we can assess how compatible they are for the long haul, what they think about each other, and why they have certain quarrels over and over again.

Values and pursuits determine compatibility in long-term relationships in accordance with the following four principles:

Principle of Bonding. Researchers have conducted many studies evaluating whether people are attracted to others who have similar versus opposite traits, and the results show that we naturally bond to people whose values and pursuits are similar to our own. As the saying goes, " Birds of a feather flock together".

Principle of Separation. The "opposite attracts" analysis is intuitively appealing but invalid. We naturally distance and separate from people whose values and pursuits are significantly different from our own. You are incompatible with people who hold opposite values and basic desires. Although complementary skills and abilities can be helpful to partnerships, opposite personality traits, values, or motives lead to conflict.

"Birds of a feather flock together" is among the most strongly validated principles in all of psychology.

Significant differences in intrinsically held values motivate quarrels that rarely resolve. University of Washington psychologist John Gottman observed that 69 percent of marital conflicts are perpetual (Gottman & Silver, 1999). "Time and again, when we do four-year follow-ups of couples, we find that they are still arguing about precisely the same issue. It is as if four minutes have passed rather than four years" (Gottman & Silver, 1999, pp. 129-130).

Principle of Self-Hugging. I came across George Ramsay's 1843 book on the nature of happiness when I was working on a research project in the library stacks at The Ohio State University. The pages were discolored and brittle from more than 150 years of exposure to the elements, but I did my best to read as much as I could. The following passage caught my attention:

> "The same difference of feeling and dullness of imagination in men explain what often has been observed, that one half of mankind pass their lives in wondering at the pursuits of the other. Not being able either to feel or to fancy the pleasure derived

from the other sources than their own, they consider the rest of the world as little better than fools, who follow empty baubles. They hug themselves as the only wise, while in truth they are only narrow-minded."

I have pondered the meaning of these words for years. I now suspect that George Ramsay – an obscure, nineteenth-century Professor of Philosophy at Oxford University in England – successfully unlocked the psychological secrets of long-term relationships. His idea of "self-hugging," I now believe, explains why people with opposite pursuits tend to misunderstand each other and quarrel repeatedly. Because of its significance, let's take a close look at what he wrote and what it meant.

1. **WHAT HE WROTE**: "The same difference of feeling and dullness of imagination in men explain what often has been observed, that one half of mankind pass their lives in wondering at the pursuits of the other." **WHAT IT MEANS**: We tend to misunderstand people who pursue interests we do not enjoy. **EXAMPLE**: The spender and saver misunderstand each other. The spender enjoys shopping, but the saver thinks it unwise and possibly even irresponsible. The saver enjoys putting money in the bank and counting it, but the spender thinks it foolish to deny oneself happiness. Saving is a joy to the miser but a frustration to the shopper. Spending is a joy to the shopper but makes the saver feel uncomfortable. Hence, each is baffled by the choices of the other.

2. **WHAT HE WROTE**: "Not being able either to feel or to fancy the pleasure derived from the other sources than their own." **WHAT IT MEANS**: The saver and shopper are "hard-wired" dif-

ferently. The saver is incapable of feeling or even imagining the pleasure the shopper derives from spending. The shopper is incapable of feeling or even imagining the comfort the saver derives from hoarding cash.

3. **WHAT HE WROTE**: "they consider the rest of the world as little better than fools, who follow empty baubles." **WHAT IT MEANS**: People with different pursuits mark each other down. The saver thinks the shopper has chosen an irresponsible, foolish lifestyle, and the shopper thinks the same of the saver. Each thinks the other would be happier with their with their pursuits rather than the goal they pursue.

4. **WHAT HE WROTE**: "They hug themselves as the only wise, while in truth they are only narrow-minded." **WHAT IT MEANS**: When we self-discover who we are, we have a tendency to think we have learned something about human nature, rather than about ourselves. The saver thinks it is human nature to be happier hoarding essentials such as money, while the shopper thinks it is human nature to buy what is desired now. Each is proud of what they think they know. Each confuses narrow-mindedness about the other person for wisdom.

Again, self-hugging is a natural tendency to think that our values are best, not just for us, but potentially for everyone. When people learn that a particular lifestyle makes them happy, they think they have learned something about human nature, when in reality they only learned something about themselves. Sociable people think, "Socializing is fun" when they should think, "Socializing is fun for me." Intellectuals assume, "It is human nature to enjoy learning," when they should conclude, "I enjoy learning." Self-reliant psychologists assert, "Autonomy is a sign of human growth," when they should assert, "Autonomy is important for my growth."

Self-hugging is a natural tendency to think that our values are best, not just for us, but potentially for everyone.

Because of self-hugging, many not-so-happy people never doubt what leads to happiness. They think, "If only I were more successful or wealthy or better looking, I would be truly happy." Many not-so-happy people are so confident they know what leads to happiness they give advice to people who are happier than they are. A miserable intellectual can tell a happy nonintellectual, "You can't be really happy. To be really happy, you must acquire great knowledge and understanding." A not-so-happy puritan looks at a happy playboy and thinks, "His happiness is shallow. How can anybody relate to people in such a superficial manner? He would be happier if he could find deep, enduring relationships."

Self-hugging occurs with regard to our strongest and weakest basic desires. Strong basic desires motivate us to embrace strong values, which makes it more difficult for us to understand people who hold opposite values. Weak basic desires have a similar effect. Consider the example of an ambitious parent and a laid-back child. The ambitious parent asks the unambitious child, "Why don't you get a job and work harder and make something of your life?" The unambitious child responds, "Why don't you do something other than work, work, and work?" In this example, the parent has a high need for power, whereas the child has a low need for power. The quarrel is motivated by self-hugging — that is, the parent imposes his or her values on the child thinking this is what is best for the child. The child imposes his or her values on the parent, marking him or her down for working too much and not stopping to smell the roses. Conflict resolution requires that ambitious and unambitious people understand that they are individuals so that one intrinsically enjoys what the other intrinsically dislikes and vice versa. Tolerance of individuality is often the only possible solution.

> *Since human beings are naturally intolerant of people with significantly different values and pursuits, successful relationships at work or at home are typically between people with similar values and pursuits.*

Principle of Everyday Tyranny. It is best to think of human motivation as the assertion of core values, not as psychic energy. We are a species motivated to assert our values, especially our pursuits. In a relationship two people with different values and pursuits will assert themselves against each other. Through "self-hugging" each person thinks his or her values are best. Hence, they try to change the values of the other person, thinking it is for the other person's own good. I use the term "everyday tyranny" to refer to efforts to change the values of a partner or individual with whom one has a long-term relationship, such as a child or employee.

> *"Everyday tyranny" refers to a person's efforts to impose his or her values on others, believing it is for their good.*

"Everyday tyranny" refers to a person's efforts to impose his or her values on others, believing it is for the other person's good. The parent, teacher, or boss who has a gregarious personality thinks quiet people are missing out on a lot of fun. Maybe quiet people fear being rejected so they tend to keep to themselves, or maybe they lack social skills. In reality nothing is wrong with quiet people: Introverts just happen to value socializing differently than extroverts do.

In human relationships the same quarrels occur over and over. Maybe your parents used everyday tyranny to try to change you, or maybe you do the same with your partner or children. It would be a better world if we could tolerate people whose values contradict our own and stop trying to change others to be more like us.

CHAPTER 9

What People Think of Each Other

If we have the RMP results of any two people, we can apply the principle of self-hugging to estimate what they might think of each other if they worked or lived together over a long period of time. For those basic desires for which the individuals are matched — both are "high" for a particular basic desire, or both are "low" — they tend to think positively about each oher. For those basic desires for which the individuals are mismatched — one is "high" for a particular basic desire, and the other is "low" for the same basic desire — they tend to mark each other down and may quarrel repeatedly. As is generally true with the RMP, we do not interpret "average" desires.

Mismatched desires on the RMP motivate conflicts of values. A spouse with a high need for status, for example, values living in an expensive

> *Mismatched desires on the RMP motivate conflicts of core values.*

residential neighborhood, while a spouse with a low need for status might feel embarrassed or uncomfortable living in a prestigious neighborhood. They may quarrel with each other over and over on issues pertaining to prestige and status. The disagreement does not resolve easily, if at all, because it is a conflict of core values.

The following are the typical implications for matched and mismatched desires in a relationship of two people. It doesn't matter if we are analyzing a romantic relationship between two partners, or a work relationship between supervisor and employee, between two executives, or between two co-workers.

Table 9-1. What people with Matched and Mismatched Basic Desires Think of Each Other

Basic Desire	Thoughts
Acceptance is the basic desire for positive self-regard.	high/high: Both are self-confident with "can do" attitude. low/low: Both are insecure and reluctant to risk failure. high/low: Self-confident person may think insecure person requires too much reassurance or is too indecisive. Insecure person may think self-confident person is conceited or slick. Repeated quarrels over trying new things and/or risking failure.

Basic Desire	Thoughts
Curiosity is the basic desire for understanding.	high/high: Both are intellectuals. low/low: Both are practical; neither enjoys intellectual pursuits. high/low: Intellectual thinks practical person is boring. Practical person thinks intellectual is arrogant, impractical, and/or nerdy. Repeated quarrels over difficulty of understanding each other, talking too much, superficiality, and/or significance of education for children.
Eating is the basic desire for food.	high/high: Both enjoy eating. low/low: Both do not care about culinary issues. high/low: Light eater thinks hearty eater lacks willpower. Hearty eater thinks light eater denies pleasures for self. Repeated quarrels over meals, weight, and/or self-control.
Family is the basic desire to raise children and to spend time with siblings.	high/high: Both want to raise a family. low/low: Neither wants to raise a family. high/low: Family person thinks non-family person is selfish or is missing out on life's greatest joys. Non-family person thinks family person is tied down and sacrifices own life for children. Repeated quarrels over having children, raising them, and/or time spent away from home.

Basic Desire	Thoughts
Honor is the basic desire for upright character.	high/high: Both keep promises and are responsible. low/low: Both are expedient. high/low: Principled person thinks expedient person is self-serving and lacks character. Expedient person thinks principled person is righteous or sanctimonious. Repeated quarrels over issues of ethics, loyalty, and/or responsibility.
Idealism is the basic desire for social justice.	high/high: Both are concerned about fairness and social causes. low/low: Both have a realistic, hard-nosed attitude toward the injustices of life. high/low: Idealist thinks realist lacks compassion. Realist thinks idealist is a dreamer. Repeated quarrels over social causes, fairness, helping the downtrodden, and/or politics.
Independence is the basic desire for self-reliance.	high/high: Both are independent and self-reliant. low/low: Both are interdependent and rely on others. high/low: Independent person may think interdependent person is immature and/or needy. Interdependent person may think independent person is stubborn or afraid of intimacy. Repeated quarrels over issues of emotional support or stubbornness.

Basic Desire	Thoughts
Order is the basic desire for structure.	high/high: Both are orderly and tidy. low/low: Both follow their nose, resist orderliness, and are spontaneous. high/low: Organized person thinks spontaneous person is inefficient and/or disorganized. Spontaneous person thinks organized person is mired in trivia. Repeated quarrels over housekeeping issues.
Physical activity is the basic desire for muscle exercise.	high/high: Both are active people. low/low: Both are sedentary people. high/low: Active person thinks sedentary individual is lazy. Sedentary person thinks active individual is exhausting. Repeated quarrels over issues pertaining to fitness, physical exertion, and/or lifestyle.
Power is the basic desire for influence or leadership.	high/high: Both are assertive and ambitious; they value competence. low/low: Both are nonassertive and laid-back. high/low: Assertive person thinks non-assertive person is laid-back or unsuccessful. Nonassertive person thinks assertive individual works too much, is controlling, and is overly ambitious. Repeated quarrels over issues of control, how hard each works.

Basic Desire	Thoughts
Romance is the basic desire for beauty and sex.	high/high: Both are passionate people. low/low: Both have an ascetic personality. high/low: Passionate person thinks the ascetic individual is prudish, has hang ups, and/ or is self-denying. Ascetic person thinks the passionate individual is hedonistic, a pleasure seeker, non-spiritual, or focused on unimportant aspects of life. Repeated quarrels over issues pertaining to sensuality, romance, or beauty.
Saving is the basic desire to collect.	high/high: Both are collectors. low/low: Neither is a collector. high/low: Collector thinks the non-collector is wasteful and/or doesn't take care of things. The non-collector thinks the collector is a tightwad or miser. Repeated quarrels over taking care of property and/or possibly money.
Social contact is the basic desire for peer companionship.	high/high: Both are gregarious, fun loving, and interested in belonging to groups or clubs. low/low: Both are introverted, private, or loners high/low: Gregarious person thinks the introvert is shy and possibly afraid of rejection. The introvert thinks the gregarious person is superficial. Repeated quarrels over social life.

Basic Desire	Thoughts
Status is the basic desire for respect based on social standing.	high/high: Both value wealth, status, reputation. low/low: Both identify with ordinary, middle class people. high/low: Status-focused person thinks the egalitarian is unimportant. The egalitarian thinks the status-focused person is an elitist, stiff, too formal. Repeated quarrels over issues of reputation, prestige, and/or formalities.
Tranquility is the basic desire for safety.	high/high: Both are timid. low/low: Both are courageous or adventurous. high/low: Timid person thinks adventurous person is reckless. Adventurous person thinks timid person is a coward. Repeated quarrels over issues of avoiding or facing danger.
Vengeance is the basic desire to confront those who offend.	high/high: Both are competitive and confrontational people. low/low: Both are conflict avoidant; neither is competitive. high/low: Competitive person thinks conflict-avoidant person is weak and/or naive. Conflict-avoidant person thinks competitive person is angry, intimidating, and/or overly aggressive. Repeated quarrels over issues pertaining to conflict, competition, and/or confrontation.

PART III

*Applications of Reiss
Motivation Profile*®

CHAPTER 10

Self-Discovery

In the summer of 1963 following completion of my junior year in high school, I decided to take seriously Socrates's famous dictum, "Know thyself." I enrolled in an introductory philosophy course at City College of New York. One summer afternoon I sat down under a tree with my philosophy books, determined to get to know myself in a much deeper way than I had up to that point. I tried to meditate, but nothing bubbled up from inner me. I learned that it was one thing for Socrates to advise his students to "know thyself," but quite another to provide a method for attaining that goal. 'Know thyself" is easy to say but requires a method to do.

It is now almost 50 years from that hot summer afternoon where I first sat under a tree to get to know myself better. The RMP I constructed is becoming a popular self-discovery method. Like all good self-discovery methods, it makes clear what you vaguely already know but hadn't quite yet put your finger on.

Self-discovery is a process of learning who you are and how you are similar and different from other people. Psychologists have developed three methods for self-discovery, called psychodynamic, personality type theory, and human needs theory.

- Psychodynamic self-discovery purports to teach people about their unconscious thoughts and desires, and how hidden mental processes might relate to past childhood experiences. It is based on Freud's theory of mental illness.

- Personality type theory, as stated by Isabel Myers and Katherine Briggs, purports to teach people about innate tendencies for processing information and how such tendencies might determine their personality traits. Myers and Briggs claimed to be applying the mysticism of Swiss psychologist Carl Jung, who was a psychotherapist and observer of mankind.

- Human needs theory, as stated herein, purports to teach people how their personality traits arise from their intrinsic motives and core values. It is based on the study of conscious purposes as revealed by large, scientifically valid surveys of diverse groups of people.

The RMP falls under self-discovery based on needs, motives, and values. People who take the RMP learn what motivates them and how they prioritize universal goals. They gain insight into how their motives and values play out in relationships - at work/school or at home.

The RMP can help us self-discover our personality "blind spots," which are qualities that are obvious to everyone who knows us but which we somehow overlook. Consider the example of Barack Obama, who bragged about multitasking. He boasted he could walk while chewing gum. On the RMP, he likely would obtain a below average score for the basic desire for order. A blind spot motivated by a low need for order is not noticing when others think you are doing too much. Shortly after he became president, Obama started a myriad of new projects, everything from overhauling health care to a new national energy policy. He was blind to the simple fact that he was pursuing too many projects at the same time. He thought he was impressing others by showing them how many good ideas he has and how competent he is. He was slow to realize that many observers expected him to fail because he was trying to do too much too soon.

Remember when presidential candidate John Kerry offered nuanced answers to questions to contrast himself with the incurious President George W. Bush? Kerry was blind about how difficult it was for ordinary people to understand what he was saying. Bush's political team successfully attacked him for being too intellectual and confusing.

On the other hand, presidential candidate Mitt Romney has a personality blind spot pertaining to the assertion of the values motivated by the basic desire for status, such as wealth and social standing. Psychologically, his statement about not caring about 47 percent of the population is about the link between status and attention. (See my blog, "What I leaned from Prince Charles.") We pay attention to people with high status, but we ignore those with low status.

The RMP often is compared with the Myers Briggs Type Indicator (MBTI) because both tools are used to teach tolerance of diverse personalities. The message of the MBTI is that we are very different from each other in terms of how we perceive things and organize our energy. The differences are so great we often misunderstand each other, which leads to unnecessary conflicts and other problems. We need greater understanding and greater tolerance of individuals with personality types not our own.

The RMP is used to teach a similar lesson. We are individuals to a greater extent than is commonly appreciated. One individual values work, but another values leisure. One values adventure, but another values caution. Through greater understanding and tolerance, we can significantly reduce personality conflicts, which can consume significant resources, time, and energy.

The MBTI fares poorly against essential scientific criteria. Many behavioral scientists have questioned the validity of the MBTI (Barbuto, 1997; Garden, 1991; Girelli & Stake, 1993; Hunsley et al, 2003; Pittegner, 1993). The tool has been negatively evaluated by both the United States Army and by the Education Testing Service (e.g., Pettingger, 1969). The main problem is the lack of evidence for the 16 personality types the MBTI is supposed to assess. Some of the 16 types may not exist.

Another limitation of the MBTI is its focus on a narrow range of motivational personality traits, especially orderliness, sociability, and intellectual curiosity. The MBTI lacks comprehensiveness because it has no or few items regarding a number of relevant aspects of personality such as parenting, status, romance, physical activity, achievement, competitiveness, and saving. The MBTI's theoretical foundation is based on too few personality dimensions to provide a detailed explanation of the normal personality.

Although the RMP is more comprehensive than the MBTI, the two instruments are compatible when used jointly for self-discovery. Both instruments are embedded in a message of tolerance of all kinds of personalities, which is so important for teamwork and relationships. Both teach self-awareness. To facilitate the self-discovery process, I recommend the joint use of both instruments because two instruments can stimulate people to think more deeply about who they are. When the two instruments are used together, individuals can compare their results and choose which ones they think best describe them. The RMP is the superior tool when scientific rigor is essential, but the MBTI still has educational value, and the use of the two tools together stimulates people to think about commonalities and discrepancies between the two sets of results.

Alexander Steinmetz, the former head of human resources at Schott Corporation, is certified as a master with both the RMP and the MBTI. In a paper entitled "RMP versus MBTI: Comparison Application in Consulting and Training," Steinmetz compared his experiences with the two instruments used jointly. He found that after clients use both instruments for a while, most come to favor the RMP and eventually stop using the MBTI. He also found that the RMP is significantly superior to the MBTI when used to assess stress on the job and when the focus is on conflict resolution. At the team level the RMP was particularly easy for the team members to understand. Finally, most people who take both tools liked the fact that the RMP scale is quantified as continua, whereas the MBTI scores force an either/or choice.

CHAPTER 11

Motivation in Business

As summarized in Table 11-1, the 16 basic desires have been applied to business by life coaches and business consultants especially Dr. Maximilian Koch in Austria; Dr. Thomas Mengel in Canada; Peter Boltersdorf and Alexander Steinmetz in Germany; John Delnoy in the Netherlands; Dr. Alexey Kornilov in Russia; Joanne Lee and Kelvin Lim in Singapore; Daniele and Bruno Gianella in Switzerland; and Dr. Jody Simpson in the United States.

LEADERSHIP TRAINING.

The RMP is used in leadership training programs for purposes of enhancing emotional intelligence, self-awareness, and/or human development. It may add to, or replace, training based on Maslow's theory of motivation and/or Myers Briggs personality types.

Mengel (2012) discussed a model for integrating the 16 basic desires with Viktor Frankl's (1965) search for meaning. In a paper entitled "Living, Learning, Leadership – Motivation in the Context of Identity Development of Undergraduate Students," Mengel (2011) administered the RMP to a class of 25 students in a university-based leadership training program. He also conducted focus groups and surveys to assess the students' opinions on the profiles. He learned that 62% found the RMP to be "rather or very accurate". As the following comments suggest, the RMP helped some students to better understand themselves:

> It forced me to think about myself. It was kind of an awaking. Mine said I have a high need for order and physical activity, and I know that, if I don't make a list or don't plan my day, it isn't productive. Or if I don't do physical activity for a few days, I get really down in the dumps. This year lately, I've been ignoring these basics needs and the profile reminded me. It was a reminder...of who I am.

> When we first read this book I did not fully understand why we were learning it, therefore I decided not to take the test in the model. However, when we were shown the results in class and when I saw how every person is different from the rest of the people I was very impressed. Interested of what I saw that day in class, I went back and I did the test in the book to find out more about what the profile would say about me. After doing the assessment I was surprised to see the results, I learned many things about myself that I didn't know before, for example I scored very high on power. I also learned things about myself

that I knew I had but never really wanted to admit to myself, for example I scored really low on saving. The Reiss Profile® also turned out to be really accurate; which is something that I highly doubted when I first read about the profile. The Reiss Profile® helped me identify several aspects of my personality and it also helped me recognize how unique I was from other people. I believe that I was very lucky to be introduced to this book and to have the opportunity to assess myself through this profile.

EXECUTIVE COACHING.

The RMP is the centerpiece of a new strategy for coaching people at work. This new method is both quick and accurate, often leading to inexpensive, practical solutions.

Many adjustment problems can be analyzed in terms of the "fit" between the individual's needs and values, on the one hand, and the demands of the work or home environment, on

> *The RMP is the centerpiece of a new strategy for coaching people at work. This new method is both quick and accurate, often leading to inexpensive, practical solutions.*

the other hand. Typically the needs that are particularly difficult to satisfy are those that depart the most from the norm. In other words, our strongest — and our weakest — basic desires are the ones most likely to cause us problems at work or home.

When a person has a problem at work, for example, the RMP Master looks at the individual's most important basic desires and determines if any are mismatched to the work duties or work team. A business coach reported the example of a business owner who experienced selling as stressful and who wasn't very good at it. The results of the individual's RMP showed a low need for social contact, indicating that he is an introvert who dislikes small talk. He needs to hire someone else to sell his product because he or she will never do it well.

A friend of mine supervised a doctor who excelled in his professional skills but worked at a pace that was too leisurely. He had a high need for curiosity, which motivated him to acquire exceptional knowledge within his field, and a low need for power, which motivated him to value leisurely pursuits and basically not work as hard as top professionals are expected to do. The supervisor encouraged him to change jobs. He became a supervisor of students, which he could pursue without working unusually hard. He was successful at his new post.

Tom is a workaholic. He is always working, seemingly 24 hours a day, seven days a week. He enjoys work, but it causes problem at home with his wife and children. The likely motive driving his behavior is a very high need for power (achievement), possibly combined with a low need for family. The solution depends on what other needs might motivate Tom to work less and to pay more attention to his family. The solution begins, however, with everyone understanding that it is an extreme need for achievement, not a mental illness, that motivates Tom to work so much.

CONFLICT RESOLUTION.

The RMP is used for conflict resolution aimed at enhancing team functioning. Typically the life coach or psychologist administers the RMP to the individuals who are in conflict with each other. They then meet to develop a deeper understanding of the issues and to discuss their differences. Here is an example supplied by Dr. Andy Dix, who works for a large telecommunications company. Dr. Dix titled this case example, "Misunderstanding Motives Kills Teamwork."

> Tom was embarrassed when he discovered a few typographical errors in the advertising proposal he had just given to a client. Tom confronted Sally about the errors, saying he had relied on her to create an error- free presentation, and now he felt he could no longer trust the quality of Sally's work.
>
> Sally was visibly shaken by this confrontation and went to her manager's office to complain about what she felt was Tom's inappropriate outburst and criticism of her.
>
> The manager spoke with both Tom and Sally about the incident, but both parties were defensive and thought they should have been treated with greater respect. Each was uncertain if he or she could work together any longer.
>
> The manager contacted a Reiss Motivation Profile® Master, who administered the RMP to Tom and Sally and conducted an individual debriefing session with each person. Tom discovered that he has a low need for independence. To achieve his sales goals, he thought he needed a team of trusted professionals surrounding him, much like Navy Seals trust each other with their lives when on a dangerous mission. He felt that Sally did not care as much about her job as he did, and that her carelessness shows she is unreliable. From the RMP Tom could see that his lack of trust in Sally frustrated his need for interdependence.

The results of Sally's RMP revealed high needs for acceptance, power, and status, plus an average need for independence. During her profile debriefing, she explained how she had been dealing with a considerable amount of personal doubts in her abilities in her new role. She felt intimidated by Tom, and that his expectations were unreasonable. She felt she was personally under attack when Tom confronted her and that he was being disrespectful and unreasonable. She became very upset because she felt like she had failed in her new role and that her boss would now think of her as a failure. Her feelings of being unfairly judged had overwhelmed her and she had begun to cry.

The RMP Master asked Tom and Sally to rank each other's needs from a summary description of the 16 basic desires. With the permission of both parties, the RMP Master then shared the other's actual RMP. They both had scored the other person's motives to be similar to his/her own and had missed the key differences in motives that had contributed to the misunderstanding.

The RMP Master facilitated a group discussion with Tom, Sally, and their manager aimed at achieving mutual understanding. Tom and Sally learned what was most important to each other and how both of their misunderstandings had contributed to the incident. Action plans and job expectations were created and agreed on by all of the participants. Tom agreed to provide more positive feedback on what he liked about proposals created by Sally, and she let him know how she would be most comfortable in being approached regarding errors and revisions to proposals.

Tom agreed to set aside time to check proposals for errors prior to presenting them to clients. Sally agreed to communicate more often in-person with Tom to keep him posted on her progress working on his proposals.

The pair has worked successfully together for the past three months and now speak freely to each other about their needs based on the RMP. They both report high levels of cooperation and satisfaction with their working relationship.

Alexander Steinmetz, a human resource expert and business consultant, has pioneered the use of the Reiss Motivation Profile® to lessen conflicts arising from interpersonal misunderstandings and dislikes. As an example of his work, we will consider the case study of Daniel and Christa, who work in an office of eight sales managers.

David and Christa need to work in close cooperation to serve their customers. They are peers who both report to the managing director. One Monday Christa approached her boss to report that she will resign if she has to work with Daniel in the future. She has had sleepless nights, worrying that she cannot serve customers properly given the chaotic work environment.

Christa complained that with Daniel everything is done at the last minute, with no proper planning. When she tries to voice her concerns, Daniel responds only that everything is on its way and there is no reason to worry. He encourages her to just stay calm even when they are unprepared to meet with clients.

On the other hand, Daniel complained that Christa is overly concerned and inflexible. She often becomes overwhelmed and emotional, which he does not like. He believes that things are under control.

So who is right?

- What is the root cause of the conflict?
- What is the dynamic in the conflict?
- How can the conflict be resolved?

Steinmetz asked both employees to complete the Reiss Motivation Profile®. The results revealed that Daniel has high needs for curiosity and independence as well as low needs for social contact, order, vengeance, tranquility, status and acceptance. His score on the need for power was at the high end of the normal range.

The RMP results also revealed that Christa has high needs for order and tranquility as well as low needs for power, curiosity, social contact, and idealism. Her score for vengeance was at the high end of the normal range.

Based on these RMP results, Steinmetz formulated answers to questions #1 and #2.

1. **The root cause** of the problem is due to different work styles. Christa's low need for curiosity motivates her to be pragmatic and unimpressed with creative ideas, while her high need for order motivates her to be detail-oriented and to value preparation and planning, with no interest in last-minute action and unforeseen changes. Her high need for order is why she describes Daniel's disorganized manner as, "This man creates chaos."

   On the other hand, Daniel's low need for order motivates his spontaneity, while his almost high need for power motivates his need for success. He values flexibility, enjoys multi-tasking, and is a last-minute person who manages to always deliver. He pays attention to details when necessary but is not keen on project management, which he views as paperwork that distracts from the solution. He says Christa is over-exact and inflexible.

Thus, the results of the RMP reveal a conflict of personality, values, and goals, all motivated by high versus low valuations in the need for order.

2. **The dynamics** of the conflict start with Christa's becoming worried about not meeting the time lines and not having the solution ready (high need for order). Both are introverts (low need for social contact) and thus are easily misunderstood as not caring about people when in reality they just do not value small talk. Christa talks to Daniel primarily when she is worried and can't sleep. Daniel likes harmony (low vengeance), is fearless and rarely worries, and is confident things will work out (low need for acceptance). When Daniel reacts confidently and calmly, Christa feels that he does not take her seriously and becomes even more angry (almost high need for vengeance).

3. What was done to **solve the conflict**? Steinmetz promoted greater mutual understanding, which defused the conflict by reducing the tendency to take personally each other's behavior. Daniel started to appreciate Christa's needs for structure and proper planning. Christa learned that Daniel actually is not chaotic; he just has a different work pattern including a high capacity to handle ambiguity. She also realized that his self-confidence is not arrogance.

Steinmetz encouraged them to communicate more often, pointing out that each is shy because of a low need for social contact and thus has a tendency to communicate less often than is needed. They established formal, regular routines to share more information.

Steinmetz used his knowledge of their motives to clarify their responsibilities. Christa was put in charge of project management. She planned the projects, set the time lines and made sure that everything was on track. She also was allowed to remind Daniel of any delays or missing details. Communication with customers was shared between them depending on the topic. So how did Daniel react when Christa was put in charge of project management, leaving him to focus on the customer solutions and the conceptual work? Very positively! Why wasn't he offended? He is low on the need for order and thus does not enjoy detail-oriented project management, and he is high on the need for curiosity and thus likes thinking of new solutions for customers.

This case example shows how the RMP can be used to analyze motives and their impact on work style, personality traits, and interpersonal relationships. Describing the conflict in terms of human needs serves to defuse the situation through the encouragement of mutual understanding. People who understand each other's motives and values can learn to get along even when they have different needs.

HIRING.

When used as a pre-employment tool, the specific profile best suited for a job would depend on the specific tasks and on other details of the job. Generally, the Honor scale should be interpreted as a measure of potential loyalty to the company; the Acceptance scale as a measure of potential for dissatisfaction and complaining; and the Interdependence scale as a measure of team spirit.

CHAPTER 12

Motivation in Schools

Motivation is the missing piece in the assessment batteries schools use to evaluate their students. Educators erroneously assume that all students were born with the potential to enjoy learning and thus schools do not have to devote much effort to motivating students. The reality is that some students are motivated in directions other than classroom learning. Even among the intellectually curious, moreover, individuals differ widely in what interests them. Boredom in the classroom is a significant limitation on what students learn.

The Reiss School Motivation Profile (RSMP) is used to assess what motivates middle and high school students. It is an adaptation of the RMP designed to be quicker than the tool used with adults. It includes only 13 of the 16 basic desires (all except eating, saving, and romance). This reduces the total number of questions from 128 to 104, and it eliminates all questions about sex, which are inappropriate for a school administration.

SIX REASONS FOR POOR GRADES

The RSMP may be used to assess the following six common motivational reasons for poor grades.

Reason 1. Fear of failure (high scores on RSMP Acceptance scale). Some students do poorly in school because they do not try hard or give inconsistent effort. Typically these students have an above-average fear of failure (as indicated by high scores on the RSMP Acceptance scale). Since they expect to fail, they hold back effort (e.g., Atkinson & Feather, 1966). They may try hard on easy tasks but not when challenged. Further, they respond poorly to criticism. When teachers or parents criticize them, they may tune them out and not hear what is being said to them. They do poorly when criticized, yelled at, or evaluated. These students may be at their best when parents and teachers stand behind and encourage them.

> The RSMP may be used for these purposes:
>
> *Assess what motivates academic underachievement (poor grades).*
>
> *Assess a student's motivation for violence.*
>
> *Assess a student's interests in future careers. (See Chapter 15.)*

Reason 2. Incuriosity (low scores on RSMP Curiosity scale). Some students do poorly in school because they hate thinking. They are willing to do only token amounts of studying in order to understand things.

The concept of incuriosity is unpopular. Educators have viewed curiosity as a natural joy, something that potentially motivates everybody. They have suggested that teachers need to tap into the natural curiosity of their students in order to motivate them. I disagree with this viewpoint. I believe that the learning process can be frustrating, especially when deep thinking is required. Although it feels good once we understand something, the learning process itself isn't necessarily joyful. Students vary enormously in how long they are willing to think about something in order to understand it. By definition, incurious students dislike the learning process, especially deep or sustained thinking.

> *The vast majority of students referred to school psychologists have a high score on the acceptance scale.*

Reason 3: Lack of Ambition (low scores on RSMP Power scale). Lack of ambition is a third motivational issue that can lead to poor grades in school. These students may be laid back or nondirective. They don't work hard enough to do well in school. They tend to score low on the RSMP Power scale.

Students with low RSMP Power scores typically do not apply themselves. They set modest goals and avoid challenging courses because they do not want to work hard. Non-ambitious students who are smart still may earn average or even above average grades, but only when they can do so without working hard.

These students may be willing to work at a moderate pace but no harder. When pushed to work hard, they may quit. They may want to avoid the most challenging courses, but they may do well in moderately challenging courses. What is "challenging," or "moderately challenging," of course, depends on the student's potential. After graduation from school, these in-dividuals may continue to avoid hard work. They may have a tendency to underachieve their entire lives, not because they are incapable, but because they are motivated in different directions.

Reason 4. Disorganized (low scores on RSMP Order scale). Students who score low on the RSMP Order scale tend to be disorganized. They may do poorly in school because some teachers mark them down for carelessness, inattentiveness to detail, and sloppiness.

Further, these students may have too many balls in the air to do any one of them well. They may start a new activity before they finish the current activity. Some of them need to learn to stay focused on a single course of action, completing one task before moving on to the next. These students are at their best on unstructured tasks and in loosely organized environments or on tasks with flexible rules.

Reason 5. Combativeness (high scores on RSMP Vengeance scale). Combative behavior is an important cause of underachievement throughout life. These individuals make enemies of potential friends. Combative school children get into fights on the playground, school cafeteria, school hallways, bathrooms, or even in the classroom itself.

These students may be at their best in competitive situations. When a student is inappropriately combative, parents and counselors should teach the difference between socially appropriate competition and inappropriate aggression or confrontation. Some (not all) students with high RSMP Vengeance scores have anger management issues.

Reason 6. Lack of Responsibility (low scores on RSMP Honor scale). Students with character issues underachieve when they are caught cheating, shirk their duties (e.g., do not do homework), or when teachers mark them down for character shortcomings. These students may need teachers to impose strict ethical limits. They may need to learn that their teachers and parents will not allow them to get away with anything and that people who cheat are likely to be caught and punished. Typically they will play by the rules when it is to their advantage to do so, but left to themselves they will cheat.

Assessing Potential for Violence. The RSMP of a potentially violent student is as follows.

- Students with very high scores on the Vengeance scale value revenge. These students have strongly endorsed statements like these: I try to retaliate when attacked. When I get angry, I strike back.

- Students with high scores on the Acceptance scale are unusually sensitive to rejection, which is a possible trigger for aggression. These students have strongly endorsed statements such as: I worry that others will find fault with me. I have great difficulty dealing with rejection.

The combination of high vengeance and high acceptance indicates increased likelihood of aggression, possibly violence. Uncommonly high sensitivity to rejection, combined with very high valuation of revenge, provides an impetus for aggression or violence. For such a person, attention seeking might drive the aggressive impulses toward dramatic action. Conversely, the occurrence of average or low scores on the vengeance scale suggests aggression is unlikely.

Other scores on the RSMP that are relevant to the prediction of violent behavior include:

1. An above average score on the Status scale suggests a strong need for attention. A number of recent school shooters in the USA were seeking attention.

2. A very low score on the Tranquility scale means the student is not afraid of being hurt. The absence of aggression anxiety, which inhibits acting on violent impulses, is likely to be common in students who exhibit violent behavior. On the other hand, high scores on this scale predict timidity, which would be counter indicative to the expression of aggressive behavior.

3. A very low score on the Honor scale means the student does not care about right and wrong, whereas a very low score on the Idealism scale means the student lacks compassion for others. Low scores on these two scales suggest minimal moral inhibition against the expression of violent behavior.

Like all psychological tools, the Reiss School Motivation Profile® is not valid in every case. School psychologists should use this tool as one part of an overall assessment.

CHAPTER 13

Relationship Counseling

D r. Stephen Judah, a Columbus marriage counselor, and I created the Reiss Relationship Profile (RRP), which assesses the compatibility between any two individuals. It is simply a comparison of the RMPs of two individuals.

A "matched" basic desire is strong (high) for both individuals or weak (low) for both individuals.

A "mismatched" basic desire is strong (high) for one person but weak (low) for the other.

The results of the RRP include the "Incompatibility Index" score, which is the total degree of dissimilarity of basic desires. [It is the sum of the absolute values of the difference scores.] The higher the Index score, the greater is the potential incompatibility of the couple. How many mismatches signal an unhealthy relationship? Although five or six mismatches may spell significant trouble, the couple must decide for themselves when the strengths of the relationship outweigh the weaknesses or vice versa. The RRP is just a tool for helping people make decisions and possibly improve their relationship.

The RRP assesses compatibility, not romantic love. The results show the areas of life where the partners are pulling in the same direction versus those where they are pulling against each other. Part of what makes relationships so complicated, I suspect, is that a person may fall in love with someone with whom they cannot get along.

Some basic desires may be more important than others in determining the outcome of a romantic relationship. Orderly and spontaneous people may quarrel over housekeeping matters, but these quarrels rarely spell significant trouble for a marriage. On the other hand, couples who quarrel over whether or not to have children and raise a family have a significant problem. No compromise is likely to resolve this difference.

Sexual compatibility is obviously very important for a successful marriage. When one partner wants to have sex much more frequently than the other, the stage is set for repeated frustration, quarrels, infidelity, and acts of revenge. The passionate partner may complain that the ascetic partner is only infrequently interested, and the ascetic partner may complain that the passionate partner has a one-track mind.

Assessing Intimacy. Many married people complain that their partner is reluctant to share feelings, or talk about the relationship in an emotionally supportive and close manner. Sometimes such problems can be understood in terms of an incompatibility in the need for independence. The partner who seeks more emotional support may have a low need for independence, whereas the partner who avoids being emotionally close may have a high need for independence.

Independent people typically dislike being in need of others, which for some includes not wanting to need others for emotional support. Some highly independent people may be reluctant to express gratitude for favors because acknowledging their need for assistance calls attention to their interdependence. Many independent people dislike touchy-feely experiences. Independent people are less likely to be religious, presumably because they do not want to rely on anybody, not even on God.

In contrast, interdependent people are comforted knowing they can rely on others to meet their needs. They are typically motivated to seek out intimidate or close relationships. Many interdependent people value touchy-feely experiences or emotional closeness, or they may seek to become one with their partner.

In a relationship, the independent and interdependent partners are each motivated to gratify their own needs, which necessarily frustrates their partner's needs. The independent person is motivated toward self-reliance, which may include limiting the extent of emotional dependence on a spouse. Over time this person may minimize close emotional self-disclosures. The interdependent person is motivated toward emotional closeness in the relationship, which makes the independent person uncomfortable.

Due to self-hugging, the independent person thinks the interdependent partner is "weak" because he/she needs others. The interdependent partner thinks the independent partner has hang ups that wall off his or her feelings and need for intimacy. Each wonders what is wrong with the other. The couple may quarrel repeatedly over issues of emotional closeness, stubbornness, dependency, and not talking about feelings. The independent person may complain that the interdependent partner is too needy, immature, or burdensome, and the interdependent partner may complain that the independent partner does not provide sufficient emotional support, is too cold, or is insensitive.

Most people show both independent and interdependent traits. Sometimes they are self-reliant, but at other times they rely on their partner or significant others. People who show both independent and interdependent behaviors at different times typically have an average need. It is primarily when a person's need for independence is strong that he/she may exhibit a general avoidance of closeness. It is only when a person's need for independence is weak that he/she exhibits a general neediness.

Assessing Infidelity. Two of 16 basic human needs — romance and honor — are relevant to understanding fidelity versus cheating in romantic and marital relationships.

To understand how romance may impact likelihood of infidelity, I apply the "Principle of Strong Needs," which is original with the theory of 16 basic desires. This principle says that the number of desired gratification objects increases as does the strength of a person's need. A person with a hearty appetite, for example, tends to eat everything, whereas a person with a weak appetite tends to eat like a bird. A curious person wants to learn about everything, whereas an incurious person wants to learn about only one or two favored topics. A gregarious person (high need for social contact) befriends everybody, whereas a private person (low need for social contact) seeks only a few close friends. People with a high need for status usually buy the most expensive items, whereas those with a weak need for status aren't impressed with material possessions.

By applying the Principle of Strong Needs to sex, we expect people with strong sex drives to seek many partners, whereas those with weak sex drives to seek few. This prediction will not hold every time–there are numerous people who have a high sex drive and are loyal to their spouse–but I think it predicts both cheating and promiscuity much better than any other method I know.

People with strong sexual needs may seek multiple partners, but that does not mean they are reckless. I think it is invalid to say that former President Bill Clinton was "reckless" just because he had extramarital sex and got caught. The construct "strength of need" predicts promiscuity; I doubt if measures of "recklessness" add anything to such predictions. The needs for sex and risky behavior are largely unrelated. Further, I believe the trait of recklessness can be inferred only when it is manifested generally in the person's life, not just from sexual behavior alone.

Further, the basic desire for honor has implications for infidelity. People with a strong need for honor may believe that their word is their bond and, thus, they typically take marriage vows seriously. They take pride in being "promise keepers." Married people with both strong needs for sex and honor will seek to gratify their sexual desires within the marital bedroom. In contrast, expedient people believe there is nothing wrong with breaking promises when opportunity presents itself. These people have little moral inhibition regarding cheating on their partner.

Here is how the theory of 16 basic desires predicts the likelihood a married person will cheat on his or her spouse.

- Strong Need for Sex, Weak Need for Honor = high likelihood of infidelity.

- Strong Need for Sex, Strong Need for Honor = above-average likelihood of infidelity.

- Weak Need for Sex, Weak Need for Honor = below-average likelihood of infidelity.

- Weak Need for Sex, Strong Need for Honor = significantly low likelihood of infidelity.

CHAPTER 14

Sports and Wellness

When I published my book *Who am I?* in 2001, readers suggested to me the relevance of the 16 basic desires for sports, yet it was not apparent how to make the connections. Peter Boltersdorf, a German business consultant and athletic coach, made the first successful application to sports. Boltersdorf became interested in the 16 basic desires after reading a report about them in a Belgium newspaper. After meeting with me, he set out to apply them to sports. Peter's first use of the RMP in sports was with the minor league professional soccer team in Mainz, Germany, which was struggling in mid-season, largely because of poor performance from a star player. Peter determined that the player had a "high need for acceptance" and further noticed that the Mainz coach constantly berated the player during games, yelling, "Kick it right! Kick it right!"

Since a player with a high need for acceptance will only be discouraged by criticism, Peter advised the coach not to yell at him while a game was in progress. Instead, the coach should provide calm, constructive criticism after the game. The player's performance improved dramatically, and the team went on to win a division title and move up to a higher league.

When Peter told me of his consult, I gained new insights into how to apply the 16 basic desires to sports. By relating each basic desire to specific athletic tendencies, I could see that a player with a low need for honor, for example, might have a tendency to commit penalties. A player with a high need for status might perform best against a high status opponent. In total, I deduced scores of sports-specific implications from my knowledge of the 16 basic desires.

I later evaluated the needs of each player on an NCAA Division I baseball team, NCAA Division I golf team, and NCAA Division III soccer and tennis teams. The results showed dramatic differences in what motivated the various teams. The Division I players were primarily motivated by competition and achievement, whereas the Division III players—that is, those from smaller schools—were primarily motivated by social experiences. In other words, Division I athletes wanted to win, but those playing in Division III (at least the ones we assessed) wanted to make friends.

After evaluating each player's needs, I interviewed him or her one-on-one. I might say to a baseball player, for example, "The results of my assessment suggest that you have a tendency to perform better on game day than in practice. We know my assessments are often invalid; in your case, do you play better on game day than during practice?" Despite the invitation to disagree with my assessment of their basic desires, we found that the athletes agreed with about 85% of the tendencies suggested to them.

We then consulted separately with the players' coaches, who also agreed with the vast majority of the results. By the end of the year, the Division I golf team finished sixth in the nation (the best performance in the history of the university) and the baseball team showed modest improvement over the previous year. (We did not ask the Division III teams for performance outcomes because their stated goal was participation, not winning.)

We executed a scientific study aimed at identifying a motivational profile for athletes (Reiss, Wiltz, & Sherman, 2001). We administered the RMP to 415 college students who had participated in zero, one, or two or more varsity sports at high school or college levels. How many different sports a student participated in was found to be associated the basic desires for physical exercise, social contact, family, vengeance, power, and curiosity. Based

Athletes tend to be family-oriented.

on the results of this study, the motivational profile for athletes generally is active (high physical activity), sociable (high social contact), family-oriented (high family), competitive (high vengeance), achievement-oriented (high power), and practical or non-intellectual (low curiosity).

Perhaps the most notable finding was that athletes are family-oriented. This has proven to describe not only our research samples in the USA but also Boltersdorf's assessment of professional and world-class amateur athletes in Germany. Generally, the best approach for coaches to motivate their team is to give emphasis to their status as role models for children.

Today the theory of 16 basic desires offers new methods for sports psychology. Our current model uses the 16 basic desires to suggest:

- What motivates each athlete;
- What are the athlete's tendencies (such as leadership, inconsistency, penalty-prone);
- How each athlete is likely to relate to the coaching staff (what specifically each athlete likes and dislikes about each coach; what specifically each coach likes and dislikes about each player).

Boltersdorf has had significant success using these methods. One of his teams won a world championship in handball while playing before a large international television audience. He consulted with a major league professional soccer team, which played in a national championship game. Matthias Steiner, with whom Peter consulted, won a gold medal in weightlifting at the Beijing Olympics in 2008.

After the 16 basic desires were applied to sports, we applied them to wellness. Everybody knows how to pursue wellness – eat nutritious food in moderation and exercise regularly. Yet many people have inadequate motivation to follow on a daily basis a sensible a plan for healthy living. We designed the Reiss Motivation Profile® for Wellness to help individuals seeking methods for boosting motivation for fitness and healthy living.

The Reiss Motivation Profile® for Wellness and the Reiss Motivation Profile® for Sports differ only in terms of the interpretive report accompanying the results. The interpretive report for RMP Wellness is a plain-language commentary on how best to motivate oneself for healthy eating and physical exercise. It discusses, for example, whether to exercise alone or with friends, in a gym or outdoors, and it offers tips for controlling appetite based on one's personality. It is available directly to the public at www.16desires .com. The Sports version is available to the public at www.iaimtowin.com.

CHAPTER 15

Career Counseling

The RMP is well suited as a tool for career counseling. A skilled RMP master can match individuals to potentially satisfying jobs. Here are the suggested careers for each basic desire. (Please note that in the business version of the RMP, a scale assessing the basic desire for beauty is substituted for the romance scale so as not to ask questions about sex. Further, in the business version the scales assessing the basic desires for honor and independence are reversed scored.)

ACCEPTANCE

<u>High Striving</u>. Some people with a high need for acceptance might do well in jobs or careers with infrequent evaluations such as church worker, civil servant, some public school positions, small business owner, garden-

er, truck driver, and any corporate position where there is a friendly, supportive, or non-judgmental supervisor. They may dislike working in a job that requires self-confidence or exposure to frequent criticism — such as sales, politics, research scientist, or actor — or working for any supervisor who is judgmental and quick to criticize others.

Low Striving. Some people with a low need for acceptance do better than most people at jobs that involve frequent evaluation, rejection, or criticism. Examples of such jobs are sales, telemarketer, politics, writer, actor or actress, and research professor. Some might be motivated in jobs involving adventure, such as travel to exotic or foreign lands.

BEAUTY

High Striving. Some individuals with this need may do well in jobs requiring artistic skills, design, grace, taste, or the use of color. Possible examples include architect, beautician, dancer, designer, fashion model, naturalist, and florist.

Low Striving. Some people with this need are poorly suited to a job or career that rewards attentiveness to beauty, design, or sensuality. Possible examples include architect, beautician, dancer, designer, fashion model, and florist. Compared to the average person, these individuals might tolerate jobs that require exposure to unattractive or austere environments or situations such as working in an inner city or an oil field.

CURIOSITY

High Striving. Some curious people might be interested in a career or job that is intellectually stimulating. Examples include astronaut, business executive, detective, editor, engineer, investor, journalist, lawyer, librarian, nurse, scientist, and teacher. On the other hand, they might be disinterested in a career or job that requires minimal intellectual effort such as animal caregiver, assembler, barber, carpenter, data entry person, factory worker, hair stylist, garment worker (sewing), painter, repair person, truck driver, typist, and waiter.

Low Striving. Some practical people might be interested in a career or job that requires common sense and practical knowledge. Possible examples include assembler, barber, carpenter, construction, hair stylist, factory worker, farmer, firefighter, garment worker, police officer, mechanic, painter, gardener, and waiter. On the other hand, they might wish to avoid jobs that require deep thinking or knowledge of many topics such as business executive, detective, editor, engineer, investor, journalist, lawyer, librarian, nurse, scientist, and teacher.

EATING

High Striving. Some hearty eaters might be interested in a career or job that requires knowledge of foods, food preparation, diet, and/or eating habits. Possible examples include cook, caterer, supermarket manager, taster, and restaurant manager.

Low Striving. Some light eaters might be interested in a career or job that rewards being thin such as fashion model, dietician, or weight loss professional. Since light eaters tend to be relatively inattentive to issues relevant to food, however, they are at a disadvantage learning a career or job having to do with food, food preparation, and/or eating habits. Possible examples of the jobs they should think about carefully before accepting include caterer, cook, supermarket manager, taster, and restaurant manager.

FAMILY

High Striving. Family-oriented people might be interested in a career or job that is relevant to children, families, or pertaining to nurturing plants and animals. Some of the many examples include athlete, camp manager or attendant, daycare attendant, farmer, hotel management, housekeeper, household worker, pediatric nurse or physician, personal attendant, politician, real estate agent, or teacher. They might be especially interested in work that still leaves them plenty of time to devote to their family, such as part-time or work-at-home jobs.

Low Striving. Non-family-oriented people might be interested in a career or job that has little to do with children. Some of the many examples of such careers and jobs include business executive, factory worker, military soldier, night watchman, and stock/commodity trader.

EXPEDIENCE (HONOR)

Low Need for Expedience/High Need for Honor. Conscientious people might be interested in a career or job that give emphasis to integrity, character, or loyalty. Possible examples include clergy, judge, scientist, teacher, and umpire. On the other hand, they might be uncomfortable with any career or job in which they would be expected to cut corners or produce a shoddy product for profit.

High Need for Expedience/Low Need for Honor. These individuals may be interested in a job or career that gives emphasis to self-interest or taking advantage of opportunities. Examples include businessperson, entrepreneur, investor, and stock or commodity trader. On the other hand, they might be disinterested in a job or career in which employees are expected to help others without a clear benefit in return. Possible examples include humanitarian worker, volunteer, community worker, and military service.

IDEALISM

<u>High Striving</u>. Idealists might be interested in a career or job that gives emphasis to helping people, improving society, or promoting fairness. Possible examples include alternative energy (solar, wind) employee, civil servant, clergy, community organizer, environmentalist, judge, physician, social worker, and umpire. On the other hand, they might be uncomfortable with a career or job in which they would be expected to act against the interests of the poor, needy, or downtrodden. Possible examples include auditor, bill collector, diplomat, and mortgage foreclosure server.

<u>Low Striving</u>. Realists might be interested in a job or career that rewards their hardnosed attitudes. Possible examples include auditor, banker, bill collector, chemical plant worker, diplomat, investor, polluter, repossessions, and Wall Street trader. On the other hand, they might be uncomfortable with any career or job that rewards idealism. Possible examples include community organizer, civil servant, social worker, and environmentalist.

INTERDEPENDENCE (INDEPENDENCE)

<u>High Need for Interdependence/ Low Need for Independence</u>. Interdependent people might be interested in a career or job that provides

a high degree of teamwork or emotional sensitivity. Possible examples include clergy, counselor, middle management, personal attendant, and salesperson. On the other hand, they might dislike a career or job that requires a high degree of independent decision-making. Possible examples include entrepreneur, small business owner, and Wall Street trader.

Low Need for Interdependence/ High Need for Independence. Independent people might be interested in a career or job that provides a high degree of freedom and decision-making. Possible examples include book author, commodities trader, entrepreneur, investor, small business owner, and Wall Street trader. On the other hand, they might dislike a career or job that requires a high degree of teamwork or emotional sensitivity. Possible examples include clergy, counselor, middle management, personal attendant, and salesperson.

ORDER

High Striving. Orderly people are at their best in any position where their duties are clearly specified, their supervision is constant and predictable, and they spend time organizing, scheduling, planning, or implementing rules. They might be interested in a job or career that rewards attention to details, procedure, organization, repetition, or cleanliness. Possible examples include accountant, cleaner, clerk, editor, lawyer, nurse, office manager, pharmacist, physician, tax examiner, and waiter. On the other hand, they might be disinterested in a job or career that rewards flexibility or spontaneity. Possible examples include advertising, air traffic controller, consultant, creative writer, gambler, ombudsmen, and Wall Street trader.

<u>Low Striving</u>. Flexible people might be interested in a job or career that that rewards spontaneity and/or capacity to cope with ambiguity. Possible examples include advertising, air traffic controller, consultant, creative writer, gambler, ombudsman, and Wall Street trader. On the other hand, they might be poorly suited for a job or career that rewards attention to details, procedure, organization, repetition, or cleanliness. Possible examples include accountant, cleaner, editor, housekeeper, lawyer, negotiator, nurse, office manager, physician, and waiter or waitress.

PHYSICAL EXERCISE

<u>High Striving</u>. Active people might be interested in a job or career that rewards strength, stamina, fitness, or athletic skills. Possible examples include athlete, athletic trainer, flight attendant, firefighter, mover, police work, soldier, and waiter or waitress. On the other hand, they might be disinterested in a job or career that involves a lot of inactivity such as computer technician, desk jobs, judge, university professor, or Wall Street trader.

<u>Low Striving</u>. Inactive people might be interested in a job or career that involves little physical exertion. Possible examples include announcer, book author, clerk, editor, computer programmer, investor, and web designer. On the other hand, they might be disinterested in a job or career that requires strength, stamina, fitness, or athletic skills. Possible examples include athlete, police work, firefighter, military, mover, and waiter or waitress.

POWER

High Striving. Willful people might be interested in a job or career that rewards leadership ability and/or hard work and is challenging. Possible examples include builder, entrepreneur, executive, lawyer, manager, military officer, politician, and scientist. On the other hand, they might be disinterested in a job or career that doesn't challenge them or that consists mostly in assisting or backing up others. Possible examples include clerk, flight attendant, executive assistant, ghost writer, laboratory technician, and secretary.

Low Striving. Nondirective people might be interested in a 9 to 5 job or career that does not require taking work home and permits a lot of time off for leisure. Possible examples include bank teller, clerk, dental assistant, government worker, laboratory technician, office worker, military soldier, and secretary. On the other hand, they might be disinterested in a job or career that rewards leadership ability. Possible examples include entrepreneur, executive, lawyer, and politician.

SAVING

High Striving. Collectors may be at their best working in jobs that reward frugality or collecting such as warehouse manager, museum curator, financial officer, banker, hobby store owner, rare coin or stamp dealer, repair or maintenance worker, handyman, or used car/merchandise dealer. They may be frustrated in positions in which free spending is common such as purchasing agent, retail chain buyer, defense procurement, and waste disposal.

Low Striving. Non-savers may like jobs where things are disposed of or where they can buy things. Examples include purchasing agent, retail chain buyer, defense procurement, and waste disposal. They may be frustrated in jobs where frugality or saving is rewarded such as financial officer, banker, repair person, handyman, or rare coin collector.

SOCIAL CONTACT

<u>High Striving</u>. Sociable people might be interested in a job or career that rewards social skills and interest in other people. Possible examples include civil servant, counselor, flight attendant, interviewer, marketer, party planner, public relations, recreation chief, recruiter, and salesperson. They might dislike a job or career that involves significant time alone. Possible examples include book author, night watchman, painter, security guard, truck driver, or any job in a remote, isolated place such as a researcher in Antarctica.

<u>Low Striving</u>. Private people are at their best in any job or career requiring only infrequent contact with other adults. Possible examples include working at home, working in rural areas, book author, night watchman, security guard, truck driver, postal delivery, or researcher in Antarctica. They might be poorly matched to a job or career that involves significant social contact. Possible examples include civil servant, counselor, interviewer, marketer, party planner, public relations, recreation recruiter, and salesperson.

STATUS

<u>High Striving</u>. People with a strong need might be interested in a job or career that is prestigious. The prestige may be associated with the job

itself, the employer, the cost of the product, or even the location. Possible examples include athlete, dentist, diplomat, executive, investment banker, jewelry salesperson or shop owner, lawyer, luxury car salesperson, physician, protocol officer, and stockbroker. They might dislike any job or career associated with the working class or lacking prestige. Possible examples include assembler, builder, claims adjuster, data entry technician, department store sales, factory worker, funeral director, mechanic, nanny, painter, repairman, and taxi cab driver.

<u>Low Striving</u>. People with a weak need might be interested in a job or career that is associated with the working class. Possible examples include assembler, builder, claims adjuster, data entry technician, department store sales, factory worker, funeral director, mechanic, nanny, painter, repairman, and taxi cab driver. They might dislike any job that involves interacting with wealthy or formal people. Possible examples include diplomat, investment banker, salesperson of luxury goods, and protocol officer.

TRANQUILITY

<u>High Striving</u>. Cautious people might be interested in a job or career that gives emphasis to safety and involves little stress. Possible examples include barber, builder, carpenter, florist, forester, funeral director, housekeeper, janitor, librarian, nutritionist, painter, and repair person. They might dislike stressful jobs or careers, or those that require exposure to danger. Possible examples include athlete, bill collector, air traffic controller, bomb/ hazardous material squad, policeperson, security guard, soldier, surgeon, and travel agent.

Low Striving. Many brave people are at their best in any position where performance under stress or danger is relevant to job performance. Possible examples include athlete, bill collector, air traffic controller, bomb/hazardous material squad, electrician, nurse, policeperson, security guard, soldier, surgeon, trader, and travel agent. They might dislike a job or career that gives emphasis to safety and involves little stress. Possible examples include barber, builder, carpenter, clergy, florist, forester, funeral director, housekeeper, janitor, librarian, nutritionist, painter, and repair person.

VENGEANCE

High Striving. Some people with a strong need might be interested in a job or career that gives emphasis to competition, protection, or confrontation. Possible examples include advocate, agent, athlete, bill collector, business executive, coach, entrepreneur, lawyer, prizefighter, security guard, and soldier. They might be disinterested in a job or career that gives emphasis to gentleness, conflict avoidance, or resolution. Possible examples include daycare worker, judge, negotiator, and teacher.

Low Striving. Some of these individuals may be well suited to jobs or careers that require cooperation with other people. Possible examples include daycare worker, judge, negotiator, and teacher. On the other hand, they may be disinterested in a job or career that gives emphasis to competition, protection, or confrontation. Possible examples include advocate, agent, athlete, bill collector, business executive, coach, entrepreneur, lawyer, prizefighter, security guard, and soldier.

CHAPTER 16

Marketing

A number of companies have explored the use of the RMP for advertising and marketing. Since the RMP online questionnaire has been translated into most European languages and into a number of Asian languages, it offers advertisers a single measure that can be used to study brands, advertisements, and products on a multinational basis.

A scientific method for evaluating the motives and values associated with a product was exemplified in a 2004 article I published with James Wiltz, titled "Why People Watch Reality TV." We asked 239 adults to rate themselves on the RMP and to complete a questionnaire on how much they watched and enjoyed reality television. We computed the average RMP scores for three groups of people: those who liked zero, one, or more than one show. The results revealed a correlation between how much people valued status and how much they liked reality television. The basic desire for status expresses the values of materialism, wealth, fame, and popularity, which seem to account for some of the appeal of reality television.

As in the Reiss and Wiltz (2004) study, marketers can use the RMP to identify the key values motivating interest in a product or brand. The method is to administer the RMP to three groups of respondents who vary in how much they like the product or brand. The basic desires that vary systematically with valuation of the product are the ones likely motivating interest. The values associated with these basic desires are the ones likely associated with the product or brand.

In recent years three large multinational companies have used the RMP in advertising. As is a common practice in the advertising field, these studies are covered by privacy agreements that prohibit me from identifying the companies or (to the extent I know of them) the results.

An apparent problem with online marketing research is the extent to which the respondents are providing valid answers versus simply rushing through the questionnaire. The RMP Confirmation Scale (see Chapter 21) can be used to eliminate the responders providing random answers.

The 16 basic desires permit us to compare the values expressed by a brand with those expressed by advertisements. Consider, for example, the advertisement, "What happens in Vegas, stays in Vegas." This slogan expresses the value of expedience, which is motivated by a weak need for honor. The value here is not to get caught. Since the brand for Las Vegas is "sin city"—sin falls under low honor—the advertising slogan is a direct hit on the value of the brand. In other words, the advertisement is "on message."

Here is another example of an advertisement that captures the values associated with the product. For many years Nike's slogan was, "Just Do It!" In terms of the theory of 16 basic desires, this slogan expresses the values of a person who has a low need for curiosity. The product, of course, was sneakers. As a group, athletes consistently have low curiosity on the RMP. Thus, the slogan "Just Do It" appeals to the values of the target audience.

CHAPTER 17

People with Special Needs

My colleagues and I constructed a psychometric instrument for assessing the human needs and life motives of people with intellectual disabilities over the age of 11. This tool is completed by parents, teachers, or caregivers. It is called the "Reiss Profile IDD."

This work is especially relevant to planning the future of a person with an intellectual disability. The instrument encourages caregivers to focus on what makes the individual a unique person; that is, on who the individual is, and what he or she needs for a satisfying life. The results of this assessment offer numerous suggestions for improving quality of life and for enhancing happiness for each individual evaluated.

Analysis of human needs makes it possible to replace the language of disability (e.g., "person with intellectual disability") with the language of individuality (e.g., "friendly person"). Assessment of human needs provides new and powerful methods for training caregivers to recognize the human qualities of each individual they serve and to stop thinking of their clients in terms of categories of disabilities.

CHAPTER 18

Religion and Spirituality

In Zygon, a peer-reviewed academic journal devoted to science and religion, I published an original scientific theory on how the 16 basic desires play out in religion (Reiss, 2004). I plan to expand on these ideas to encourage scientific research on religious experiences and to support the application of the 16 basic desires to faith-based counseling.

The theory of 16 basic desires offers an original, scientifically testable theory of religion. Premise 1 is the search for meaning gives rise to religion. Premise 2 is that the 16 basic desires are 16 elements of meaningful human experience. If Premises 1 and 2 are both valid, as I believe, we should expect to find numerous connections between the 16 basic desires and religious practices and beliefs. As expected, religion in fact addresses all 16 basic desires.

1. **Human beings perceive God as the greatest imaginable expression of at least 13 of the 16 basic desires.** The human images of God are about universal goals valued by everyone. These images model what is meaningful in human life. Here is how I connect divine attributes with basic desires.

- Savior, an expression of the basic desire for acceptance. I contend that salvation is the greatest imaginable approval.

- Omniscient, an expression of the basic desire for curiosity. Omniscience is the greatest imaginable knowledge.

- Love, an expression of the basic desire for family.

- Moral, an expression of the basic desire for honor.

- Just, an expression of the basic desire for idealism.

- Self-sufficient, an expression of the basic desire for independence. Nothing can be imagined to be more self-sufficient than God.

- Eternal, an expression of the basic desire for order.

- Almighty, an expression of the basic desire for strength (physical activity).

- Creator, an expression of the basic desire for power. Creation is the greatest imaginable achievement.

- Friends, an expression of the basic desire for social contact.

- Divine, an expression of the basic desire for status. Divinity is the highest imaginable status, higher even than royalty.

- Protector, an expression of the basic desire for tranquility. Divine protection provides the greatest imaginable safety from harm.

- Wrathful, an expression of the basic desire for vengeance.

The three basic desires not expressed by the Judeo-Christian images of God are eating, romance, and saving. The Judeo-Christian God does not eat, marry, or hoard vital supplies. Nevertheless, church life provides the faithful with activities to gratify these basic desires. Religious dietary laws, for example, provide guidance for the management of the basic desire for eating. The Roman Catholic Church views itself as the Bride of Christ, and in some orders nuns dress as brides for their investiture. The Church sells relics and various religious items for collectors. Between dogma and church life, religion addresses all 16 basic desires, so that individuals can gratify all of their needs through active participation in their religion.

We shouldn't think of these as "projections" of human desires, the way Freud did, but as expressions of values. It shouldn't surprise us that the attributes of God would be qualities everyone values. If it were otherwise, it would be impossible psychologically for people to worship God.

2. **Nearly every religious story, symbol, or experience expresses one or more of the 16 basic desires**. Creation, for example, expresses the basic desire for high power; the Ten Commandments express he basic desire for high honor; and the Sermon on the Mount expresses the basic desire for low vengeance. In aggregate, religious beliefs, practices, and symbols address all of the 16 basic desires of human nature.

3. **Religious Self-Discovery**. With completion of the RMP, it is possible for religious individuals to gain insight into their attraction

to religion. In Table 18-1, I summarize the RMP results for one of our research volunteers, Emma. I consider her to be a religious person partially because she visits her church at least twice a week, sometimes as often as four times a week, and she prays daily. At the time of the assessment, she was a 63 year-old mother of two and grandmother of four.

Table 18-1. Reiss Motivation Profile for Emma

High Needs (Strong Desires)	Average Needs	Low Needs (Weak Desires)
Eating	Acceptance	Curiosity
Honor	Independence	Physical Activity
Idealism	Order	Power
Family	Romance	Status
Saving	Tranquility	Vengeance
Social Contact		

The results of Emma's RMP show that she has six strong desires and five weak desires. Here is how these basic desires play out in her religious life.

When asked about her most vivid religious memories, Emma replied "Being married in the church, having my children baptized in church, and seeing my grandchildren in church and attending the same Sunday school that I attended. Funerals touch me because of the promise of eternal life." Note that her most vivid memories are mostly about her family, which was one of her strongest needs/desires. Emma's participation in religion helps her fulfill her desire for family and reinforces her family values. She stated, "We are all part of the church family, and having the same religion is a unifying force."

Emma lives in an inexpensive rural area and struggles to make ends meet. When an earthquake struck Haiti, she went to church, prayed for the victims, and donated money to her church's fund for Haitian victims. She turned to her religion to express her compassion, which falls under her high desire for idealism.

Emma accepts the Bible as historical truth. She believes in the Devil and has basically a fundamentalist approach to religion. This is consistent with her low desire for curiosity; she does not intellectually challenge what she is taught about God and religion. The single exception is that she does not believe in the wrath of God, which is consistent with her low desire for vengeance.

COMPOSITE MOTIVATION PROFILE OF RELIGIOUS PEOPLE

Religious and secular organizations offer different lifestyles and activities for satisfying our needs. We have a need, for example, to educate our children. We can send them to public school or to religious school. Our children have a need for positive social experiences. We can encourage them to attend dances at a public school or at a church school. We have a need for altruism, which we can satisfy by giving to secular or religious charities.

We have considerable freedom of choice in how we satisfy our needs. At least in democratic societies, people can be as religious or as nonreligious as they choose. Nobody can order me to support my religion or attend religious services. I live as I choose, much like everybody else living in a democratic society.

Why do some people satisfy their needs through mostly religious activities while others do so through mostly secular activities? Maybe it depends on the particular needs of the individual. Perhaps people with certain motivation profiles are more likely to turn to religion to satisfy their needs, while those with other motivation profiles are more likely to embrace secular activities.

Is there a particular desire profile associated with being religious? To explore this fascinating issue, we asked 558 adult Americans from diverse backgrounds to complete the RMP and to rate how religious they are: very, somewhat, not at all, or atheist (Reiss, 2000). Because of the small number of atheists, we combined the "not at all" and "atheist" categories into a "not religious category." The four largest denominations represented in the sample were Catholic (n=171), Methodist (n=54), Baptist (n=44), and Presbyterian (n=44). The average age was 33 (range 18 to 83).

Table 18-2. Composite RMP for Very Religious People

Above Average	Average	Below Average
Family	Acceptance	Independence
Honor	Curiosity	Romance
Idealism	Eating	Vengeance
Order	Physical Activity	
	Power	
	Saving	
	Social Contact	
	Status	
	Tranquility	

The results are presented in Table 18-2. The religious Christians who participated in the study place above average valuation on honor (morality), family life, idealism (charity), and order (ritual). They place below average valuation on independence, romance (sex), and vengeance.

The study suggested that the desire for honor may be the single most important psychological motive of the religious people who participated in the study. Honor motivates loyalty to ancestors as well as character development. People with a strong need for honor are loyal, responsible, trustworthy, righteous, and self-disciplined. In contrast, those with a weak need for honor are expedient and opportunistic. The results imply that religion appeals to a significantly larger percentage of honorable people than to opportunists.

Religion appeals to honorable people because it consistently supports their values. Religion is steeped in tradition and provides many reminders of ancestors. It teaches morality to the young. It encourages worshipping a moral God and rejecting the Devil, who is pure evil. It praises the moral self-discipline of saints and ascetics.

In contrast, religion offers very little support for those who have only a weak need for honor; these individuals value opportunism and expedience. Religion has nothing good to say about expedience, disloyalty to parents or ancestors, lying, and so on. People who pride themselves on their skills for taking advantage of opportunities that come their way may view many religious teachings as rejecting their values. These people may turn to secular activities — finance, business, or sports — to find support for their values.

The results of our study also suggested that religious people place below average value on the basic desire for independence. Why are religious people more *inter*dependent-minded than are nonreligious people? Perhaps because independent people do not enjoy having to rely on anybody, not even God. They may be reluctant to pray to God for a favor. They may be stubborn or may insist on doing things their way. They may be given to displays of individuality or pride.

The religious people in our study showed an above average need for family. Christian churches consistently preach the virtues of family values. They encourage young people to marry and to raise children within the faith. They offer social activities for families. In contrast, they offer very little or no support for those who want to remain single or for married couples who do not want to have children. I know of no religious stories or myths in which a couple who chooses not to have children is praised by God or church for their decision.

Further, we found that religious Christians placed a much lower value on confrontation and aggression, and a much higher value on cooperation and gentleness, that did nonreligious Christians. This result is consistent with Christ's teaching to "turn the other cheek." Christianity strongly supports the values of gentle people, which suggests that it might appeal to these individuals more than it does to aggressive people.

To summarize, the motivation profile of religious Christians that emerged from the study included high needs for family, honor, idealism, and order, plus weak needs for independence, romance (sex), and vengeance. This profile suggests that Christianity should appeal particularly well to people who place high value on morality, family life, gentleness, and connectedness. Religious teachings consistently support these values while offering less or little support for people with opposite values.

The motivation profile of the clergy may differ from that of the flock. In a survey of 49 Protestant seminary students, Havercamp (1998) found a very high need for idealism. Apparently, young Christian seminary students in the Havercamp study, all of whom were men, were motivated by the ideal of making the world a better place.

Is Spirituality a Personality Trait?

Should the list of 16 basic desires be expanded to include spirituality as a seventeenth basic desire? As was noted previously, it is not uncommon for people to look at the list of 16 basic desires and ask, "Where is spirituality? What about God and religion?"

I believe that people relate to God through a comprehensive array of basic desires, not through a single mode of contact, or separate dimension of personality called "spirituality." The 16 basic desires represent the 16 dimensions of meaningful experience. For example, I believe that the faithful are connected to God through their basic desire for family when they sit down for a difficult conversation with a rebellious child. They are connected with God through their basic desire for honor when they care for their sick and aging parents. They are connected to God through their basic desire for intellectual stimulation when they are curled up in a chair reading philosophy. *God is there for everyone who seeks him. He doesn't just work for the faithful when they meditate and pray. He inspires them 24/7.*

Religion is not the seventeenth basic desire, as some have suggested. If I had recognized spirituality as a seventeenth striving, this would imply that a person's spirituality is separate and distinct from the rest of his or her life. As my theory stands today with no striving for spirituality, I assert that human beings have 16 basic desires or needs, and they are free to gratify all, some, or none of those needs through religious or spiritual activities, versus all, some, or none of those needs through secular activities. God has given human beings 16 significant needs and left us free to choose religious or secular lifestyles to gratify those needs. I believe that religion addresses all aspects of life, not just a single need or personality trait.

Please note that the explanations of the theory of 16 basic desires are scientifically testable, which is unusual for a scholarly theory of religion. The desires are assessed objectively by a standardized psychological measure. Since the measure is independent of the religious phenomena it may explain, there is no circularity at all.

FAITH-BASED COUNSELING

Looking forward, the 16 basic desires could strengthen faith-based or pastoral counseling. Clergy and faith-based counselors help many millions of people cope with life problems such as marital conflict, child rearing, and alcoholism. The 16 basic desires support new counseling methods that are quick and easy to apply; it is possible for the counselor to be helpful after only a few short sessions. Further, these methods address the counseling needs of ordinary people, as distinguished from mentally ill people.

PART IV

RMP User Manual

CHAPTER 19

RMP Administration, Scoring, Norms

The results of the RMP are insensitive to minor changes in methods of administration. The RMP typically takes 10-15 minutes to complete. It can be administered online or as a paper-and-pencil questionnaire. It can be administered in individual or group format. The important points to make when administering the test are these:

- The individual should rate each item, leaving no blanks.
- The individual needs to make the ratings on his or her own without consultation or conversation with anyone else.
- The RMP has no right or wrong answers.

If an individual does not understand a question, or asks for the definition of a term, the test administrator should instruct the client to rate the item "O" (zero) for a "neutral" rating.

The RMP Confirmation Scale, which is optional, is administered after all of the items on the RMP have been answered.

The instructions for the test are as follows:

> *Below are a number of statements that refer to your goals, wants, and values. Please rate the extent to which you agree or disagree with each of these statements. If the item asks about something that has not happened in your life, try to imagine how you would react if the event did happen. For example, if you do not have children and are asked how much you enjoy raising children, answer on the basis of how much you think you would enjoy it if you had them. If you are confused, have no opinion, or you neither agree nor disagree, use the "0" or "Neutral" rating.*

Individual de-briefing interviews are strongly recommended and are a standard of practice when the RMP is used in self-discovery, counseling, or business. The examiner reviews the results with the individual and discusses what they might mean. The individual is asked if he or she agrees or disagrees with each finding of a strong or weak basic desire. When agreement is indicated, the examiner may ask for examples of how the indicated motive or trait plays out in the individual's everyday life. When disagreement is indicated, the examiner may explore with the individual why he or she disagrees with the result. Here are some examples of how these conversations might go:

> De-Briefing Instructions: *The results of the RMP are statistically valid, which means that some are valid, and others are invalid. I am hoping you could help me by identifying which results you*

think might be invalid. The results suggest that you might dislike exercising or exerting yourself physically. Is that valid? Do you have a tendency to conserve your energy?

A standard of practice is to provide individual de-briefing sessions.

ONLINE SCORING

In order to discourage unauthorized use, the scoring methods and norms for the RMP are not published. The only way to score the test is online. This must be done even when the client has completed a paper-and-pencil version of the test.

The initial norms were based on 1,749 people recruited from 29 different sources located throughout the United States and Ontario, Canada. No incentives were used to encourage participation. The recruitment sources included high school English classes and psychology classes, five private or public colleges located as much as two thousand miles apart and serving ethnically diverse populations, members of two different church groups located in different states, volunteers in a community organization (Kiwanis Club), professionals from across the United States and Canada who attended a seminar on mental retardation, and residents of nursing homes.

The norms were updated and revised in 2010 based on a sample of about 30,000 people from North America, Germany, and Holland. The sample came mostly from the business world. Prior to 2013, the norms used were averages of scores for males and females. Beginning in the summer of 2013, gender and age and culture specific norms have been used based on a sample of about 60,000 people from North America, Germany, and Holland.

CHAPTER 20

RMP Reliability and Validity

The list of 16 basic desires is the only taxonomy of human needs that was both empirically derived and scientifically validated. It is based on factor studies of what diverse samples of people said motivates them. In this chapter the scientific data are summarized including reliability and validity coefficients.

In our first study, we administered a 328-item questionnaire about motives and goals to a diverse sample of 401 adults from many walks in life, and we submitted the results to mathematical analyses aimed at determining how many significant basic desires we should interpret. Based on the results of a maximum likelihood extraction method with oblique direct oblimin rotations, the first factor study yielded 15 factors, each suggesting a different motive. The initial 328-item instrument was revised significantly to support the 15-factor solution. One hundred and ten items were retained, and 110 new items were added to the instrument, so that the second draft instrument had 220 items, 108 fewer than the first draft RMP.

> *The list of 16 basic desires is the only taxonomy of human needs that was empirically derived.*

The process of factor analysis and instrument revision was repeated three times and followed with a fourth, confirmatory factor study. Each study was conducted with a different sample with no person participating in more than one study. Reiss and Havercamp (1998) and Havercamp and Reiss (2003) executed a total of six RMP factor studies (N = 2,032). The samples consisted of 401, 380, 341, and 398 people. Each sample included diverse adolescents and adults from different walks in life and various states of residence. The fourth study confirmed the 15-factor solution.

Subsequently, we executed two additional factor analytic studies intended to add a sixteenth factor, called saving, to assess the motive of hoarding. The second of these studies was a confirmatory factor analysis with a new sample of 512 adults solicited from several sources in urban and rural Ohio and Indiana. Using an oblique rotation, Havercamp (1998) found that the Steiger-Lind Root Mean Square Error of Approximation (RMSEA) was .053; the Expected Cross-Validation Index (ECVI) was 38.962; the Non-Normed Fit Index was .894; and the Normed Fit Index was .8379. These results were interpreted as indicating a reasonable fit of the 16-factor model with the data obtained in our second confirmatory factor analysis.

Researchers have presented evidence for the reliability and validity of each of the 16 RMP scales. The following is a summary of this evidence.

I have included here the statistical p values in order to show how uncommonly powerful the validity effects are. Professional experience suggests that the RMP's validity "can be seen," meaning it is evident in real-world behavior.

The successful confirmatory factor studies provided replicated evidence for the "construct validity" of the 16 basic desires.

The measures used to assess concurrent validity are as follows: NEOPIR (Big 5; Costa and McCrae, 1992); Myers Briggs Type Indicator (MBTI; Myers, McCaulley, Quenk, & Hammer, 1998); Work Preference Inventory measure of intrinsic and extrinsic motivation (Amabile, Hill, Hennessey, and Tighe, 1994); Purpose in Life (Crumbaugh & Maholick, 1964); Positive and Negative Affect (Watson, Clark, & Tellegen, 1988); Personality Research Form (Jackson, 1984); Sternberg Triangular Love Scale (Sternberg, 1998); Romantic Attractiveness Scale (Campbell, 1999) Relationship Assessment Scale (Hendrick, 1988) and Anxiety Sensitivity Index (Reiss, Peterson, Taylor, Schmidt, & Weems, 2008).

Acceptance. This scale is intended as an assessment of the fear of failure and rejection. People with high scores are theoretically predisposed to become insecure, whereas those with low scores may tend to be self-confident.

The 4-week test-retest reliability was estimated at .80. Cronbach's alpha coefficient of internal reliability was estimated at .80.

The RMP Acceptance scale is positively correlated with "Big 5" Neuroticism, $r = .50$, $p < .01$ (Olson & Weber, 2004). This finding is consistent with professional observations that high scores are common in individuals referred for psychological assistance.

RMP Acceptance scores also are positively correlated with Negative Affect, r = .46, p < .01, but negatively correlated with Purpose in Life scale, r = -.29, p < .01. These findings provide evidence for the concurrent and criterion validity of the scale.

Compared with a group of 737 people from diverse walks in life, a group of 71 athletes scored below-average on RMP Acceptance, t (806) = 9.71, p < .001, d = 1.21 (Havercamp & Reiss, 2003). Sports consultants have evaluated thousands of athletes, from high school to professional level, and report anecdotally that athletes tend to have low acceptance scores, although there are many individual exceptions. These findings are consistent with the assumption that self-confidence can be crucial for athletic success.

Curiosity. This scale assesses the need for understanding. People with high scores are theoretically predisposed to become intellectuals, whereas those with low scores may tend to be practical people. Students with low RMP Curiosity scores may be bored by traditional school curricula and intellectual activities.

The 4-week test-retest reliability was estimated at .84. Cronbach's alpha coefficient of internal reliability was estimated at .82.

The RMP Curiosity scale is significantly correlated with intrinsic motivation, r = .54 (Olson & Chapin 2007), and with Positive Affect, r = .26, p < .01 (Olson & Chapin 2007). Compared with MBTI Sensors, on average MBTI Intuitives scored .76 s.d.'s higher on RMP Curiosity, t (92) = -3.00, p < .01, d = .85 (Reiss & Wiltz, 2008). These findings provide support for the concurrent validity of the scale.

Compared with a group of 737 people from diverse walks in life, a group of 52 college philosophy majors scored very high for RMP Curiosity, t (787) = 7.20, p < .01, d = 1.06 (Havercamp & Reiss, 2003). Further, 19 of 49 (38.8%) low-achieving students scored at least .8 s.d.'s below the norm for curiosity, compared with only four of 49 (8.1%) who scored at least .8 s.d.'s above the norm for curiosity (Kavanaugh & Reiss, 2002). These findings provide support for the criterion validity of the RMP curiosity scale.

RMP Curiosity is positively correlated with Big 5 Openness to experience, r = .46, p < .01 (Olson & Weber, 2004). This finding supports the utility of the RMP scale as a research measure.

Eating. This scale consists of eight items assessing trait appetite. High scores theoretically suggest a tendency to overeat, whereas low scores theoretically suggest a tendency to eat little. The scores are positively correlated with extrinsic motivation, r = .35, p < .01 (Olson & Chapin 2007), but negatively correlated with adult age, t (1, 1713) = 4.82, d = .24 (Reiss & Havercamp, 2005). These findings provide support for the concurrent validity of the eating scale.

The 4-week test-retest reliability was estimated at .82. Cronbach's alpha coefficient of internal reliability was estimated at .80.

Compared with a group of 737 people from diverse walks in life, a group of 44 overweight adults scored significantly above-average on RMP Eating, t (779) = 4.55, p < .001, d = .71, as did a group of 55 culinary students, t (795) = 3.43, p < .01, d = .47 (Havercamp & Reiss, 2003). These findings support the criterion validity of the RMP Eating scale.

Olson and Weber (2004) obtained a .25 correlation between RMP Eating and Big 5 Neuroticism. The significance of this finding is unclear – it may mean that the Neuroticism scale taps into overeating, at least to a small degree.

Family. This scale consists of eight items assessing the individual's motivation for family life. High scores theoretically suggest strong parenting instincts, although in a small number of instances they may indicate instead attachment to siblings. In business contexts the desire to have time for one's children, as indicated by high scores, may come into conflict with certain jobs, possibly leading to work/life imbalances.

The 4-week test-retest reliability was estimated at .79. Cronbach's alpha coefficient of internal reliability was estimated at .92.

The RMP Family scale is positively correlated with Purpose in Life, r = .33, p < .01 (Olson & Chapin 2007); Positive Affect, r = .26, p < .01 (Olson & Chapin 2007); Big 5 Agreeableness, r = .22, p < .01 (Olson & Weber, 2004); and Big 5 Conscientiousness, r = .21, p < .01 (Olson & Weber, 2004). Compared with MBTI Thinkers, on average MBTI Feelers scored .82 s.d.'s higher on RMP Family, t (93) = 3.23, p < .01, d = .74 (Reiss & Wiltz, 2008). These findings provide support for the concurrent validity of the scale.

Professional experiences with thousands of high school, college, and professional athletes suggest that athletes score high on RMP Family.

A group of 133 Christians who rated themselves as "very religious" scored higher on RMP Family than a group of 86 Christians and atheists who rated themselves as "not at all" religious, t (1, 220) = -3.55, p < .01 (Reiss, 2000b). Since Christianity embraces family values, this finding provides evidence for the criterion validity of the RMP Family scale.

Reiss, Wiltz, & Sherman, (2001) tested 415 college students, finding that RMP Family scores were positively associated with the number of varsity high school or college sports the student had played, F (2, 242) = 7.7, p < .01. Professional experiences with thousands of high school, college, and professional athletes further suggest that athletes score high on RMP Family. These findings exemplify the research utility of the RMP Family scale.

Honor. This scale consists of eight items assessing strength of motivation for character and moral behavior. High scores theoretically suggest loyalty, trustworthiness, and valuation of the moral code of one's ancestors (e.g., Ten Commandments). Low scores theoretically suggest expedience, opportunism, and disloyalty. In business contexts, honorable people should be predisposed to stay with the same company for many years, whereas expedient people should be predisposed to change jobs when they perceive opportunities elsewhere.

The 4-week test-retest reliability was estimated at .77. Cronbach's alpha coefficient of internal reliability was estimated at .82.

The RMP Honor scale is positively correlated to Big 5 Conscientiousness, r = .31, p < 01 (Olson & Weber, 2004); Purpose in Life, r = .33, p < .01 (Olson & Chapin 2007); and Positive Affect, r = .20, p< .05 (Olson & Chapin 2007). The RMP Honor scale also is correlated with self-efficacy in choosing a career (Bath, 2002). These findings provide evidence for the concurrent validity of the RMP Honor scale.

A group of 137 Christians who had rated themselves as "very religious" scored .52 s.d.'s higher on RMP Honor than did a group of 86 Christians and atheists who had rated themselves as "not at all" religious, t (1, 220) = 5.08, p < .01 (Reiss, 2000b). These findings provide support for the criterion validity of the Honor scale.

Reiss and Wiltz (2004) found that RMP Honor scores were significantly lower for people who watched two or more reality television shows, F (2, 226) = 4.4, p < .02. This may mean that reality television generally expresses the values of expedient people.

> *In a sample of 49 low achieving high school students, 21 of 49 (42.9 percent) had significantly below-average RMP scores for honor, possibly because they shirked their homework and other academic duties, whereas four had significantly above-average scores (Kavanaugh & Reiss, 2002).*

Reiss and Havercamp (2005) found that RMP Honor scores increase with adult age, t (1, 1713) =10.0, d =. 70. These findings support the research utility of the RMP honor scale.

Professional experience suggests that people with conduct problems score low for honor. These anecdotal observations are consistent with Reiss's (2008) hypothesis that honor inhibits antisocial impulses.

Idealism. This scale consists of eight items assessing intrinsic valuation of public service, community volunteerism, and social causes. High scores theoretically suggest an enduring interest in social justice, whereas low scores theoretically suggest a "hard-nosed" approach to social issues.

The 4-week test-retest reliability was estimated at .69. Cronbach's alpha coefficient of internal reliability was estimated at .84.

RMP Idealism is positively correlated with Big 5 Agreeableness, r = .30, p< .01 (Olson & Weber, 2004); Big 5 Conscientiousness, r = .24, p < .01 (Olson & Weber, 2004); Purpose in Life, r =.28, p<.01 (Olson & Chapin 2007); and intrinsic motivation, r = .24, p < .01 (Olson & Chapin 2007). A group of RMP Idealists scored high on measures of passion (Engel, Olson, & Patrick, 2002). These findings provide support for the concurrent validity of RMP Idealism.

Compared with a group of 737 people from diverse walks in life, a group of 66 community volunteers scored high on RMP Idealism, t (801) = 3.31, p < .001, d = .43, as did a group of 49 Protestant seminary students, t (784) = 5.18, p < .01, d = .77. These findings provide support for the criterion validity of RMP idealism.

Independence. This scale consists of eight items assessing intrinsic valuation of self-reliance. High scores theoretically suggest self-reliance, possibly accompanied by stubbornness and/or valuation of individuality. In contrast, low scores theoretically suggest interdependence, possibly including intrinsic valuation for emotional closeness and connectedness.

Professional experience in both coaching and marriage counseling suggests that independent people can be difficult to get along with. In business contexts, high scores suggest a leadership style in which an executive makes decisions even when others may still disagree, whereas low scores suggest an executive who prefers to lead by consensus.

> *Reiss and Crouch (2005) found that 314 registered organ donors scored higher on RMP Idealism than did 169 non-donors, t (481) = 1.88, p < .03.*

The 4-week test-retest reliability was estimated at .72. Cronbach's alpha coefficient of internal reliability was estimated at .71.

RMP Independence is negatively correlated with Big 5 Agreeableness, r = -.29, p < .01 (Olson & Weber, 2004). Compared with MBTI Introverts, on average MBTI Extroverts scored 0.61 lower on RMP Independence, t (93) = -2.47, p < .05, d =0.58 (Reiss & Wiltz, 2008). These findings provide evidence for the concurrent validity of the RMP Independence scale.

In a study of religiosity (N= 558), RMP Independence scores decreased as self-rated religiosity increased, $F(2, 555) = 7.6$, $p < .01$ (Reiss, 2000b). Compared with a group of 737 people from diverse walks in life, a group of 49 Protestant seminary students scored below average for RMP Independence, $t(784) = 5.18$, $p < .01$, $d = .77$ (Havercamp & Reiss, 2003). In a study of 45 fundamental Christians and 19 atheists, Beasley and Rowell (2003) found that low independence scores differentiated these groups. These findings are consistent with the idea that religious people value

Atheists are more independent-minded than are believers.

oneness (as in becoming one with God) and with the viewpoint that some religious people may consider independence as the sin of pride. These findings provide evidence for the criterion validity of the RMP Independence scale.

Order. This scale consists of eight items assessing how much structure the individual needs to feel comfortable. High scores theoretically suggest orderliness, whereas low scores theoretically suggest flexibility and spontaneity. High scores theoretically suggest someone who is detailed oriented, whereas low scores theoretically suggest someone who is focused on the "big picture." Professional experience suggests that orderly people tend to stay the course, whereas spontaneous people tend to change directions quickly.

The 4-week test-retest reliability was estimated at .81. Cronbach's alpha coefficient of internal reliability was estimated at .87.

The RMP Order scale is positively correlated with PRF Order, $r = .60$, $p < .01$ (Havercamp & Reiss, 2003). On the MBTI, Judgers scored higher than Perceivers, $t(92) = 4.00$, $p < .001$, $d = .83$ (Reiss & Wiltz, 2008).

These findings provide evidence for the concurrent validity of the RMP Order scale.

RMP Order is negatively correlated with Big 5 Openness to experience scale, $r = -.19$, $p < .05$ (Olson & Weber, 2004), but positively correlated with Big 5 Conscientiousness, $r = .33$, $p < .01$ (Olson & Weber, 2004). RMP Order is positively correlated with Big 5 Neuroticism, $r = .33$, $p < .01$ (Olson & Weber, 2004), perhaps because the authors of the Big 5 Neuroticism scale regarded orderliness as compulsiveness. Reiss and Crouch (2005) found that 314 registered organ donors scored lower on RMP Order than did 169 non-donors, $t(481) = -3.35$, $p < .01$, $d = 0.32$. These findings exemplify the utility of the scale in behavioral research.

Physical Activity. This scale consists of eight items assessing trait motivation for physical exercise.

The 4-week test-retest reliability was estimated at .82. Cronbach's alpha coefficient of internal reliability was estimated at .89.

The scores are positively correlated with participation in varsity sports, $F(2, 412) = 33.1$, $p < .01$ (Reiss, Wiltz, & Sherman, 2001) and with Positive Affect, $r = .44$, $P < .05$ (Olson & Chapin 2007). Compared with a group of 737 people from diverse walks in life, a group of 71 athletes scored very high on RMP Physical Activity, $t(806) = 9.71$, $p < .01$, $d = 1.21$ (Havercamp & Reiss, 2003). A group of 65 ROTC military students also scored high for RMP Physical Activity, $t(800) = 6.26$, $p < .01$, $d = 0.81$. RMP Physical Activity is negatively correlated with adult age, $t(1, 1713) = 15.4$, $d = .86$ (Reiss & Havercamp, 2005). These findings provide evidence for the criterion validity of the RMP Physical Activity scale.

Power. This scale consists of eight items assessing motivation to lead and/or influence others. High scores theoretically suggest intrinsic valuation of leadership, achievement, and self-assertion. Low scores theoretically suggest a dislike for the spotlight, a lack of ambition, and nondirective behavior. Professional experiences suggest that people with high scores are hardworking, whereas those with low scores are laid back and easygoing.

The 4-week test-retest reliability was estimated at .84. Cronbach's alpha coefficient of internal reliability was estimated at .86.

RMP Power scores are positively correlated with the PRF Dominance scale, $r = .55$, $p < .01$ (Havercamp & Reiss, 2003) and with Big 5 Extraversion, $r = .39$, $p < .01$ (Olson & Weber, 2004). Compared with MBTI Introverts, on average MBTI Extroverts scored .39 s.d.'s higher on RMP Power, $t (93) = 2.06$, $p < .05$, $d = .40$ (Reiss & Wiltz, 2008). These findings provide evidence for the concurrent validity of the RMP Power scale.

RMP Power scores are positively correlated with participation in varsity sports, $F (2, 412) = 3.2$, $p < .05$ (Reiss, Wiltz, & Sherman, 2001). Compared with a group of 737 people from diverse walks in life, a group of 71 athletes scored .69 s.d.'s above the norm for RMP Power, $t (806) = -5.91$, $p < .01$ (Havercamp & Reiss, 2003). A group of 65 "Greek" college students (those participating in fraternities or sororities) also scored high, $t (350) = 0.01$, $p < .01$, $d = .78$, presumably because many Greek organizations aim to recruit campus leaders (Havercamp & Reiss, 2003). These findings provide evidence for the criterion validity of the RMP Power scale.

<u>Romance</u>. This scale consists of eight items assessing libido. All items directly ask about interest in sex (suggesting high face validity). High scores theoretically suggest a strong sex drive, whereas low scores theoretically suggest a below-average sex drive. Spouses with significantly different Romance scores tend to quarrel over sex.

The 4-week test-retest reliability was estimated at .87. Cronbach's alpha coefficient of internal reliability was estimated at .89.

The scores are negatively correlated with Big 5 Agreeableness, r = -.23, p < .01 and with adult age, t (1, 1713) = 8.33, p < .01, d = .41 (Reiss & Havercamp, 2005).

Saving. This scale consists of eight items assessing trait motivation for collecting. High scores theoretically suggest hoarding or frugality, whereas low scores theoretically suggest a tendency to spend or waste. Professional experience suggests that married couples with large differences in saving scores tend to quarrel over money/spending.

The 4-week test-retest reliability was estimated at .80. Cronbach's alpha coefficient of internal reliability was estimated at .76.

RMP Saving scores are positively correlated with extrinsic motivation, r = .30, p < .01 (Olson & Chapin 2007). This finding suggests that RMP savers tend to be materialistic. RMP Saving also is correlated with Big 5 Neuroticism, r = .28, p < .01 (Olson & Weber, 2004), and with Negative Affect, r= .26, p < .01, (Olson & Chapin 2007), perhaps because hoarding is a possible symptom of compulsive disorders.

Reiss and Crouch (2005) found that 314 registered organ donors scored lower on RMP Saving than did 169 non-donors, t (481) = -3.29, p < .01, d = .31. Apparently, some collectors hate throwing things away so much they even may not want to donate their organs after they die! This finding exemplifies the research utility of the Saving scale.

Social Contact. This scale consists of eight items assessing intrinsic interest in socializing. High scores theoretically suggest gregariousness, whereas low scores theoretically suggest a tendency to be private, shy, or a loner. Professional experiences with this scale suggest that people with high scores are fun loving, whereas those with low scores are "serious." High scores theoretically suggest someone who is people oriented, whereas low scores theoretically suggest someone who tends to keep to himself/herself.

The 4-week test-retest reliability was estimated at .81. Cronbach's alpha coefficient of internal reliability was estimated at .86.

RMP Social Contact scores are positively correlated with Big 5 Extraversion, r = .58, p < 01 (Olson & Weber, 2004). Compared with MBTI Introverts, on average MBTI Extroverts scored 1.03 s.d.'s higher on RMP social contact, t (93) = 5.16, p < .001, d = 1.08 (Reiss & Wiltz, 2008). RMP Social Contact scores also were positively correlated with Big 5 Openness to Experience, r = .20, p < 05 (Olson & Weber, 2004); Purpose in Life, r = .25, p <. 01 (Olson & Chapin 2007); and Positive Affect, r = .26, p<.01 (Olson & Chapin 2007). These findings provide evidence for the concurrent validity of RMP Social Contact.

Compared with a group of 737 people from diverse walks in life, a group of 65 "Greek" college students (those participating in fraternities or sororities) scored high on RMP Social Contact, t (350) = 2.95, p < .01, d = .41 (Havercamp & Reiss, 2003). This finding provides evidence for the criterion validity of the RMP Social Contact scale.

Status. This scale consists of eight items assessing motivation for respect based on social standing and prestige. High scores theoretically suggest intrinsic valuation of wealth, popularity, and/or social class, whereas low scores theoretically suggest disinterest in wealth, popularity, and/or social class. High scores suggest someone attentive to VIPs, whereas low scores suggest someone inattentive to titles and status within a company or industry.

The 4-week test-retest reliability was estimated at .88. Cronbach's alpha coefficient of internal reliability was estimated at .88.

RMP Status scores are associated with extrinsic motivation, $r = .42$, $p < .01$ and, to a lesser extent, Positive Affect, $r = .22$, $p < .05$ (Olson & Chapin 2007). These findings provide evidence for the concurrent validity of the RMP Status scale.

Compared with a group of 737 people from diverse walks in life, a group of 49 seminary students scored very low for RMP Status, $t (784) = -4.63$, $p < .01$, as did a group of 66 community service volunteers, $t (784) = -5.58$, $p < .01$ (Havercamp & Reiss, 2003). In contrast, a group of 65 "Greek" college students (those participating in fraternities or sororities) scored very high on RMP Status, $t (800) = 7.11$, $p < .01$, $d = .92$ (Havercamp & Reiss, 2003). These findings provide evidence for the criterion validity of the RMP Status scale. The seminary students were predicted to have low status because they shun costly things and wear plain clothes, and the community volunteers because they identify with the downtrodden. The "Greek" students were predicted to have high status because membership in fraternities and sororities often is considered an indicator of popularity.

In a group of 239 adults, Reiss and Wiltz (2004) found that RMP Status scores were positively associated with watching reality television shows, $F (2, 226) = 18.1$, $p < .01$. The values projected by these shows are fame and fortune, or the values associated with high RMP Status (Reiss, 2008).

Reiss and Crouch (2005) found that 314 registered organ donors scored lower on RMP Status than did 169 non-donors, $t (481) = -2.67$, $p < .01$, $d = .26$. This finding is consistent with the policy of not paying organ donors, which arguably expresses an anti-materialistic value. These findings suggest the research utility of the RMP Status scale.

Tranquility. This scale consists of eight items assessing sensitivity to anxiety and pain. Four of the items are from the 16-item Anxiety Sensitivity Index (ASI), which has been extensively validated in more than 1,600 published studies. The other four items evaluate sensitivity to pain, which has been shown in many studies to be correlated with sensitivity to anxiety (Reiss et al., 2008). High RMP Tranquility scores theoretically suggest timidity and proneness to future panic attacks or anxiety disorder, whereas low scores theoretically suggest adventuresome traits.

The 4-week test-retest reliability was estimated at .74. Cronbach's alpha coefficient of internal reliability was estimated at .82.

The RMP Tranquility scale is positively correlated with the ASI, r = .58, p < .01 (Havercamp & Reiss, 2003); with Big 5 Neuroticism, r = .46, p < .01 (Olson & Weber, 2004); and with Negative Affect, r = .32, p < .01 (Olson & Chapin 2007). These findings provide evidence for the concurrent validity of the scale.

> *The RMP Tranquility scale has items from the Anxiety Sensitivity Index (ASI), which has been validated in more than 1,600 peer reviewed studies.*

Compared with MBTI Introverts, on average MBTI Extroverts scored 0.36 s.d.'s lower on RMP Tranquility, t (93) = -2.22, p < .01, d = .35 (Reiss & Wiltz, 2008). This finding is consistent with previous findings that people with high ASI are prone to panic attacks. (As in agoraphobia, people with panic attacks tend to stay at home.)

Vengeance. This scale consists of eight items assessing strength of the motive to get even with people who offend. High scores theoretically suggest a predisposition toward confrontation, whereas low scores theoretically suggest a predisposition to avoid conflict and/or make peace. High scores suggest someone who is very competitive, whereas low scores suggest someone who prefers to get things done cooperatively and without confrontation.

The 4-week test-retest reliability was estimated at .86. Cronbach's alpha coefficient of internal reliability was estimated at .92.

RMP Vengeance scores are positively correlated with Big 5 Neuroticism, $r = .31$, $p < .05$ (Olson & Weber, 2004) and with Negative Affect, $r = .34$, $p < .01$ (Olson & Chapin 2007). RMP Vengeance scores are negatively correlated with Big 5 Agreeableness (Olson & Weber, 2004), $r = -.61$, $p < .01$, and with Purpose in Life, $r = -.32$, $p < .01$ (Olson & Chapin 2007). These findings provide evidence for the concurrent validity of the RMP Vengeance scale.

In a group of 558 Christians, Reiss (2000b) found that RMP Vengeance scores were much lower for people who rated themselves as "very religious" than for a less religious group, $F(2, 555) = -4.74$, $p < .01$. Consistent with findings that aggression decreases with adult age (Eron & Huesmann, 1990), Reiss and Havercamp (2005) found that RMP Vengeance decreased with age, $t(1, 1713) = 9.77$, $p < .01$, $d = .91$. These findings provide evidence for the criterion validity of the RMP Vengeance scale.

Reiss and Crouch (2005) found that 314 registered organ donors scored lower on RMP Vengeance than did 169 non-donors, $t(481) = -2.39$, $p < .05$, $d = .23$. In a sample of 49 low achieving high school students, 24 of 49 (49.0 percent) had significantly above-average RMP Vengeance scores, perhaps because combativeness leads to low achievement (Kavanaugh & Reiss, 2002). These findings exemplify the research utility of the RMP.

CHAPTER 21

RMP Confirmation Scale

As is widely recognized, people sometimes give false responses to items on psychological personality tests. They may answer questions in ways they imagine would put them in a more favorable light, such as exaggerating how honest or kind they are. They may deny unflattering qualities, such as denying being argumentative or making decisions without thinking about the consequences. Further, they may be uncooperative and deliberately provide random responses to questions, or generate responses in accordance with a pattern (e.g., answer 1,2 3, 1, 2,3, 1,2,3). Random responding, of course, leads to invalid results.

Some people fake their responses to psychological tests when they have a reason to think the information might be used against them. When tests are used to hire people, for example, job applicants taking tests are on guard, and they have a tendency to answer questions in ways they think will maximize their chances of being hired, rather than answer truthfully. On the other hand, an executive who hires a business coach is motivated to respond truthfully because it makes no sense to be uncooperative with someone you are paying to help you. Even in these circumstances, however, people may be reluctant to embrace unpleasant truths even to themselves and, thus, sometimes exaggerate their positive qualities.

Can the RMP be faked? Respondents can, of course, deliberately give random answers to any psychological test, just as they can lie during job interviews. They can check the middle option on the answer key every time simply because it is the middle option. Having acknowledged this, I think faking is less of problem with the RMP than with traditional personality tests.

> *Faking is less of a problem with tests of motivation than with traditional personality tests.*

The RMP is difficult to "fake good" because users have no idea how it works. Indeed, most psychologists do not understand how it works. It represents new ideas that require training to be understood well enough to fake good results. Further, what counts as a "good" answer on the RMP depends on the purpose of the testing. Users do not know this fact. For some jobs, for example, risk taking (low need for tranquility) might be a desirable result, but for others jobs caution (high need for tranquility) might be best.

Havercamp and Reiss (2004) found that biased responding due to faking good (called "social desirability") is very low. The Marlowe-Cowne Social Desirability Scale was developed to measure the tendency to endorse items that are culturally sanctioned and approved (such as helping out people in trouble, never intensely disliking anyone). The correlation with the RMP was assessed at .03, or virtually nil.

The RMP Confirmation Scale is designed to single out individuals who did not respond honestly, especially those who gave random responses. The 60 true-false items on the Confirmation Scale ask for endorsement of statements nobody would make if they had validly reported their motives. It is a confirmation scale along the lines of, "If you are motivated by X, the following could not possibly be true of you, so if you say it is, your responses are contradictory in ways unlikely to happen if you are responding sincerely. No person who reports low physical activity, for example, would endorse the statement, "I love participating in sports." If the person does, something is wrong. In an individual assessment, the examiner needs to execute a brief oral interview to nail down what is going on. In a mass testing, the individual's results would be discarded as untrustworthy and possibly faked.

The RMP Confirmation Scale isn't based on assumptions similar to the fake scales used in other personality assessments, such as the MMPI lie scales. Instead, it is based on the consistency of the information supplied on two different assessments of the same motives, flagging inconsistent information.

The RMP Confirmation Scale provides information on whether or not the individual taking the RMP is providing valid responses. We anticipate that the Confirmation Scale will reduce mistakes in the assessment of motivation, which we believe already are fewer than with other comprehensive assessments of personality. Although no psychological assessment always provides valid results, users consistently report that the RMP excels in its accuracy and validity.

CHAPTER 22

Reliability and Validity of RMP IDD

Since the RMP is a questionnaire, it is suitable only for individuals who can understand the items. For individuals with intellectual and developmental disabilities (IDD), facilitators can read the items and record answers for those who can understand but not read. For individuals with IDD who cannot understand the items, I constructed the Reiss Profile IDD.

Empirical Derivation. The RMP-IDD is an empirically derived rating scale completed by caregivers, parents, or teachers. The RMP-IDD Iteration I consisted of 157 items intended to assess the 10 needs of anxiety sensitivity, attention seeking, eating, frustration sensitivity, helps others, independence, order, physical exercise, positive mood, and social contact (Reiss & Havercamp, 1998). About two-thirds of the items directly referred to motives, such as "more than most people, seeks attention," and "always wants to win." Some items were written to refer to behaviors that strongly implied, but did not explicitly describe, motivation.

At a national conference on dual diagnosis (mental illness and intellectional disabilities), professionals and parents rated 199 people with IDD. Steven Reiss used the inter-item correlation matrix to develop a 162-item revised instrument, called RMP IDD Iteration II. This instrument included items intended to assess 15 needs — the original 10 minus positive mood, but plus curiosity, morality, pain sensitivity, acceptance, romance, and vengeance.

Reiss and Havercamp (1998) administered the 162-item RMP IDD to 515 people (304 men and 211 women). The age distribution was 14.6 percent, 75.5 percent, and 20.8 percent, respectively, for age groups 0-21, 22-55, and 56+. The percentage racial composition was 20.8, 1.2, 75.2, and 2.8, respectively, African American, Asian American, Caucasian, and Latino. All levels of intellectual disabilities were represented, mild (n=249), moderate (n=137), and severe/profound (n=107). This sample included 166 people without behavior disorders and 346 people with behavior disorders. The raters and consumers were recruited from eight community-based service and residential agencies located in Massachusetts, Connecticut, Pennsylvania, Ontario, Illinois, Texas, Ohio, and the United Kingdom. The raters said they had known the person they were rating for at least four months. In order to limit the extent to which the results might be influenced by any one rater, no person rated more than one individual. The raters also indicated whether or not the participants had been identified previously as having a behavior disorder.

The ratings were submitted to a series of exploratory factor analyses using the maximum likelihood extraction method with oblique rotations. The first factor analysis extracted 10 factors, the second 11, and so on up to 20 factors. Because the factor loadings for the 20-factor solution were very small, further analyses were not conducted. The 14-factor solution was the easiest to interpret; the solution accounted for 52% of the variance. A scale for social contact did not emerge from the exploratory factor analysis, but the scale was retained anyway because of its theoretical importance for people with IDD. We interpreted 15 factors and pared the instrument to 100 items.

Reiss and Havercamp (1998) conducted a confirmatory factor study on the RMP IDD Iteration 3, which had 15 scales and 100 items. The sample consisted of 438 people (248 men, 189 women, 1 unreported) from 24 states. Staff or relatives who attended a research presentation at the 1996 national meeting of the Arc of the United States were asked to provide ratings. Other raters provided services at one of the following locations — a large residential agency with headquarters in Ohio, a large residential provider of group homes in suburban Chicago, or a residential dual diagnosis program near Philadelphia. The percentage age distribution was 10.2, 78.2, and 25.0, respectively, for ages 0-21, 22-55, and 56+. The racial composition was 25 percent African American and 75 percent Caucasian. The intellectual disabilities severity levels were mild (n=150), moderate (n=137), and severe/profound (n=147). The sample included 179 people with no behavior disorder and 250 with a behavior disorder. When we allowed the factors to correlate, the 15-factor solution provided a reasonable fit to the data, RMSEA = .078. These results provided evidence of the factorial validity of the RMP IDD.

The RMP IDD ratings instrument assesses the following 15 needs:

Acceptance is the need for approval.

Attention is the need to be regarded as important (worthy of notice).

Curiosity is the need to explore and manipulate novel stimuli.

Eating is the need to consume food.

Helps Others is the need to nurture or altruistically assist other people.

Independence is the need for self-reliance.

Morality is the need to do what is right.

Order is the need to organize.

Physical Activity is the need to move one's muscles.

Romance is the need for sex.

Social Contact is the need for friends.

Anxiety (Tranquility I) is the need to be free of anxiety and stress.

Frustration (Tranquility II) is the need to be free of frustration.

Pain (Tranquility III) is the need to be free of pain.

Vengeance is the need to get even with others.

Lecavalier and Tasse (2001) translated, adapted, and validated the Reiss Profile IDD on a sample of 588 French-Canadian adolescents and adults with IDD. The ratings were submitted to confirmatory factor analysis and yielded an RMSEA of .079, indicating a reasonable fit to the Reiss and Havercamp (1998) model. For the 15 scales, the mean alpha coefficient of internal reliability was .84, and the mean inter-rater correlation was .63.

Reliability. Reiss and Havercamp (1998) conducted an assessment of test-retest reliability over a three-week period. The sample consisted of 44 individuals, 21 men and 23 women, who were receiving services from a large not-for-profit intellectual disabilities service agency with headquarters in New York. Participants' ages ranged from 22 to 79; racial composition was 86% Caucasian and 14% African American. Seventy percent were reported to have a behavior disorder. Agency psychology staff and direct care workers, who knew the person they were rating for at least eight months, completed the instrument. The r values for the 15 scales ranged from .72 to .89, with a mean of .81. The findings provided evidence of the stability of the scale scores over time.

Lecavalier and Havercamp (2004) demonstrated the stability of the 15 RMP-IDD scores for 79 individuals over an approximate three-year time period. In this study the test-retest reliability estimates were statistically significant for all 15 scales. Further, 89 percent of the raters could identify the person rated simply by examining the individual's profile.

Validity. Table 22-1 summarizes the evidence for the reliability and validity of the RMP IDD.

Table 22-1. Reliability and Validity of Reiss Motivation Profile IDD

Scale FV	FV	r	α	Validity Evidence
Acceptance	✓	.73	.86	People with acting out, aggressive or violent behavior scored significantly higher than those described as quiet (e.g., Crocker, Mercier, Allaire, & Roy, 2007). Negatively correlated with the Reiss Screen for Maladaptive Behavior, r = -.37 (Lecavalier & Tasse, 2002). Compatible roommates scored lower than incompatible roommates (Wiltz & Reiss, 2003).
Attention	✓	.82	.84	People with acting out, aggressive or violent behavior scored significantly higher than those described as quiet (e.g., Crocker, Mercier, Allaire, & Roy, 2007).
Curiosity	✓	.72	.82	Predicted quality of life six months after testing, r = .28 (Lunsky, 1999). Males with Klinefelter syndrome scored high on self-report assessment (Gerschwind & Dykens, 2004). Student with reputation for curiosity scored very high (Reiss & Reiss, 2004).

Eating	✓	.89	.90	People with Prader Willi Syndrome scored very high for RMP-IDD eating (Dykens & Rosener, 1999). People with Down syndrome scored high (Lecavalier & Tasse, 2005).
Helps Others	✓	.81	.89	People with acting out, aggressive or violent behavior scored significantly lower than those described as quiet, consistent with the hypothesis that RMP morality inhibits aggression (e.g., Crocker, Mercier, Allaire, & Roy, 2007). People with a dual diagnosis scored low on RMP IDD Helps Others.
Independence	✓	.82	.83	Face validity of items.
Morality	✓	.82	.69	People with acting out, aggressive or violent behavior scored significantly lower than those described as quiet, consistent with the hypothesis that RMP morality inhibits aggression (e.g., Crocker, Mercier, Allaire, & Roy, 2007). Males with Klinefelter syndrome scored high on self-report assessment (Gerschwind & Dykens, 2004).
Order	✓	.82	.81	People with Prader Willi and Williams Syndrome scored high (Dykens & Rosener, 1999). Compatible roommates scored lower than incompatible roommates (Wiltz & Reiss, 2003).
Physical Activity	✓	.79	.83	Predicted quality of life six months after testing, r = .24.
Romance	✓	.83	.88	Face validity of items.
Social Contact	✓	.78	.80	People with autism scored very low on RMP MR/DD social contact (Lunsky, 1999). High scores predicted quality of life six months later (Lunsky, 1999). Males with Klinefelter syndrome scored high on self-report assessment (Gerschwind & Dykens, 2004). People matched on RMP IDD social contact were more likely to become friends (Wiltz & Kalnins, 2008).
Anxiety (Tranquility I)	✓	.83	.77	Low scores predicted quality of life six months after testing, r=-.49 (Lunsky, 1999). People with a dual diagnosis scored high, r=.50 (Lecavalier & Tasse, 2002); people with autism scored high (Lunsky, 1999). Compatible roommates scored lower than incompatible roommates (Wiltz & Reiss, 2003).
Frustration (Tranquility II)	✓	.82	.88	People with acting out, aggressive, or violent behavior scored higher than those described as quiet (e.g., Crocker, Mercier, Allaire, & Roy, 2007). People with a dual diagnosis scored high on RMP IDD Frustration, r = .46 (Lecavalier & Tasse, 2002). People with Down syndrome scored low (Lecavalier & Tasse, 2005). Compatible roommates scored lower than incompatible roommates (Wiltz & Reiss, 2003).

Pain Sensitivity (Tranquility III)	✓	.79	.85	People with acting out, aggressive, or violent behavior scored significantly higher than those described as quiet (e.g., Crocker, Mercier, Allaire, & Roy, 2007). People with high total scores on the Reiss Screen for Maladaptive Behavior scored high for RMP IDD Pain, r = .37 (Lecavalier & Tasse, 2002). People with Down syndrome scored low (Lecavalier & Tasse, 2005).
Vengeance	✓	.85	.90	People with high total scores on the Reiss Screen for Maladaptive Behavior scored high on RMP IDD vengeance (Lecavalier & Tasse, 2002). People with acting out, aggressive, or violent behavior scored significantly higher than those described as quiet (e.g., Crocker, Mercier, Allaire, & Roy, 2007). People with Prader Willi Syndrome and those with Williams Syndrome scored high on RMP IDD vengeance (Dykens & Rosner, 1999). Compatible roommates scored lower than incompatible roommates (Wiltz & Reiss, 2003). People with high scores are unfriendly (Wiltz & Kalnins, 2008).

Chapter 23

RMP Versions and Translations

The RMP has multiple versions intended for use with different populations. The computer-generated interpretive reports vary: The business report discusses how the 16 basic desires play out at work, while the school report discusses how they play out in the classroom. On some versions an eight item scale to assess the desire for beauty is substituted for the romance scale to avoid asking about sex.

Here is how the versions differ any why:

1. The RMP business, school, sports, and wellness versions substitute a beauty scale for the romance scale. We ask no questions about sex in these versions.

2. The RMP school version assesses 13 basic desires, all except eating, saving, and romance. The aim was to shorten the tool for use with

the younger population by deleting basic desires with minimal implications for educational settings.

3. The basic desires for honor and independence are reversed scored in the business, sports, and wellness versions for semantic reasons. On these versions, "high interdependence" is used instead of "low independence," and "high expedience" is used instead of "low honor."

4. The interpretive test reports offer plain language comments on the implications of the results for the specific application (e.g., business, schools, etc.).

Here is a list of the RMP versions:

- Reiss Motivation Profile® for Self-Discovery is the original 128-item questionnaire. The report is interpreted for self-discovery, career counseling, and personality assessment.

- Reiss Motivation Profile® for Business includes 120 items from the original 128-item questionnaire plus eight items that assess the basic desire for beauty. The scales for independence and honor are reversed scored and are reported as basic desires for interdependence and expedience.

- Reiss School Motivation Profile®. All 104 items are from the original 128-item questionnaire. Three original scales are deleted: eating, romance, and saving.

- Reiss Motivation Profile® for Wellness includes 120 items from the original 128-item questionnaire plus eight items that assess the basic desire for beauty. The scales for independence and honor are reversed scored and are reported as basic desires for interdependence and expedience.

- <u>Reiss Motivation Profile® for Sports</u> includes 120 items from the original 128-item questionnaire plus eight items that assess the basic desire for beauty. The scales for independence and honor are reversed scored and are reported as basic desires for interdependence and expedience.

- <u>Reiss Relationship Profile</u> has the same 128-items as the original questionnaire. This version must be completed by two people before there are any results.

- <u>Reiss Motivation Profile® for Children</u>. This rating scale is completed by teachers or parents. At the time of this writing, it was still in the phase of research development.

- <u>Reiss Profile IDD</u>. This rating scale is completed by caregivers of persons with developmental disabilities including autism.

- <u>Translations</u>. The RMP originally was written and validated in the English language. It has since been translated into most European languages as well as an increasing number of Asian languages. The translations are carefully executed by native speakers and then are professionally translated back into English by Translations Aces of New York City. Discrepancies between the back translation and the original English-language test items are resolved by the author, Steven Reiss, in consultation with the professionals at Translation Aces. The translated test is then published online. From time to time the publisher monitors the test scores and makes appropriate revisions to the country-specific norms.

Translation Aces has been providing foreign-language services since 1937 when it was first founded as Bertrand Languages in New York City.

It employs a highly skilled and experienced staff of professional translators and has a network of native speakers it can call upon when needed.

CHAPTER 24

Motivation of Children

The Reiss School Motivation Profile® is limited to individuals age 12 and older. It can be used with students in middle or high school, but not in elementary school. Children under the age of 12 are not able to understand the questions. They cannot reliably self-report their goals, values, and motives.

Professor Carl Weems, special education teacher Keith Dunson, and I are studying the possibility of using teacher or parent ratings to assess the motives of children between the ages of 6 and 11. This has proven to be challenging because raters (especially parents) tend to rate children positively rather than realistically. In our research assessments, for example, the children were overwhelmingly rated as curious. Parents, in particular, had a tendency to view their children as curious.

School is a large part of the lives of elementary students. It is difficult for raters to evaluate the achievement motivation of students apart from the student's intellectual curiosity because school is the primary context in which young children have opportunities to achieve. Good learners tend to be rated as both curious and achievement motivated, while slow learners tend to be rated as neither curious nor achievement motivated. In contrast, high school students have opportunities to achieve in sports, art, and music, and they may dream of future success in business. They can easily self-report achievement motivation and intellectual curiosity as different motives.

After two unsuccessful studies aimed at constructing a comprehensive assessment of motives in children, Professor Carl Weems and I constructed an 80-item rating scale. Keith Dunson stepped forward to volunteer his assistance by collecting data from teachers. His efforts paid off. Parent ratings for 381 students, aged 3-12, were submitted to a confirmatory factor analysis.

Table 24-1 shows the results of an exploratory factor analysis. It briefly defines each of the ten scales for children, identifies the corresponding adult RMP scale, and provides the Cronbach alpha coefficient of internal reliability for the child motive. As shown in this table, the internal reliabilities for the child motivation scales are excellent. The six RMP basic desires not assessed in the child scale are eating, family, idealism, independence, romance, and saving.

Table 24-1. Internal Reliabilities of Reiss Motivation Profile for Children

Child Scale	Definition	RMP Scale	Alpha Coefficient
Acceptance	Sensitive to criticism	Acceptance	.83
Anxiety	Timid, nervous	Tranquility	.86
Character	Wants to do the right thing	Honor	.92
Competence	Achievement motivation	Power	.83
Competition	Quick to confront others	Vengeance	.85
Curiosity	Likes school	Curiosity	.92
Order	Needs structure	Order	.81
Physical Activity	Likes physical exertion	Physical Activity	.93
Popularity	Wants to be popular, seeks attention	Status	.90
Social Contact	Seeks many friends	Social contact	.86

Preliminary validity tests were executed comparing the ratings for the 86 students teachers had identified as having problems with the ratings for the remaining students. The students having problems had significantly higher scores on the Acceptance and Competition scales. The higher scores on Acceptance are consistent with experience with the RMP, in which students with psychological problems score higher on this need. The higher scores on the Competition scale are not surprising because some of the students are aggressive and get into fights.

The students having difficulty adjusting to school also scored significantly lower on motivation for competence, order, character, social contact, and curiosity. None of this is surprising. The low scores for competence and curiosity suggest a lack of achievement motivation and intrinsic motivation for school. These students are likely bored or frustrated by the school curriculum. The low score for social contact is consistent with withdrawal and problems making friends. A child with a low score for order may be sloppy.

The recent research on the Reiss Motivation Profile for Children is encouraging. Additional research, however, is needed to confirm the initial results reported here and to field test the tool.

PART V

Blogs

Blog A

Anxiety Sensitivity: Before the 16 Basic Desires

This story shows the connection between my earlier work on anxiety sensitivity and the 16 basic desires. I went from studying one individual difference in a universal reinforcement, which I called anxiety sensitivity, to studying 16.

My scientific work on human motivation began in 1979 when I interviewed Carol about her fear of heights. Carol was a secretary who worked at the University of Illinois at Chicago, where I taught. I instructed her to imagine looking down on the street from the top floor of a skyscraper. I then asked what she imagined might happen to her. Would she fall out the window? Would a plane come by and crash into the building? Exactly what, I asked, are you afraid will happen to you when you are high above the ground and looking down?

Carol said she would never make it to the top floor of a skyscraper because of her phobia. Instead, she thought she would faint in the elevator long before it reached the top floor. When I asked if she thought it is dangerous to look out a window on the top floor of a skyscraper, she responded negatively. She said she knew she would not fall to the ground. Why was she afraid of heights since she anticipated no danger or harm? It was her "fear of fear," so to speak, that was at the root of her phobia for heights. She was afraid of experiencing intense fear and fainting.

I realized that Carol's comments, if taken at face value, contradicted the conventional psychiatry of the 1970s. At the time, psychiatrists thought that people who fear heights are afraid of falling to the ground. Further, psychiatrists considered that fear to be irrational because the risk of falling is negligible. In apparent contradiction of this analysis, Carol reported that she wasn't afraid of falling from skyscrapers but of fainting. She was concerned about the consequences of experiencing fear, not about the imagined dangers of being high above the ground.

In 1985 Richard McNally and I published the theory of anxiety sensitivity to suggest that the "fear of fear" predicts the occurrence of phobias, Panic Disorder, and certain other anxiety conditions. We suggested that most people who experience stress expect to be fine once the source of the stress is resolved. The athlete who enters the game at a tense moment, for example, may experience stress, but he or she expects the stress to dissipate after the game is over. The athlete may view stress as temporarily unpleasant but doesn't think the experience poses an immediate possibility of harm. In contrast, a relatively small number of people have "high anxiety sensitivity," meaning they fear the sensations of anxiety. When people with high anxiety sensitivity anticipate experiencing anxiety or stress, they worry about heart attacks, panic, or mental illness.

At first our theory of anxiety sensitivity was widely criticized. The critics thought that the fear of fear is an unimportant consequence of phobias, not the cause. Psychiatrists thought Carol's fear of heights was caused by an unconscious conflict related to childhood experiences and repressed sexual feelings. Behaviorists thought her fear was caused by past experiences in which heights were associated with danger. Both the psychiatrists and the behaviorists believed that Carol's fear of fear was learned after she already was phobic due to other causes. They suggested that after she became afraid of heights, she learned she experienced fear in elevators, and this led to her fear of fainting.

McNally and I suggested that the fear of fear, or more specifically anxiety sensitivity, could be the cause, not just the consequence, of phobia. Carol might have acquired the notion that the experience of anxiety and fear is very unpleasant and even harmful. Perhaps she believed a pounding heart causes heart attacks, or that nervous shaking is the start of mental illness. Having acquired an unusual sensitivity to anxiety, she then might have developed a fear of most everything she thought might make her anxious. In this way her fear of fear might have led to a fear of heights.

I moved on to study the emotional life and mental health of people with intellectual disabilities. I helped to demonstrate that people with below average intelligence were vulnerable to the full range of psychiatric disorders. My research was cited to help justify the creation of hundreds of psychiatric clinics in North America, the United Kingdom, and elsewhere.

McNally continued to study anxiety sensitivity. He helped connect anxiety sensitivity to Oxford University Professor David M. Clark's theory of panic attacks and to SUNY-Albany Professor David Barlow's research on the treatment of anxiety disorders. McNally eventually persuaded the critics of anxiety sensitivity to conduct their own studies to test our predictions rather than just assume we were wrong. As of this writing, more than 1,600 studies — which is a very large number for a single topic of research — have validated the construct of anxiety sensitivity. Apart from how much anxiety a person experiences, the individual's sensitivity to anxiety predicts future fears and panic experiences. In several studies the 16-item questionnaire I wrote — called the "Anxiety Sensitivity Index" — outperformed the U.S. military's entire battery of psychological tests in terms of predicting maladjustment to basic training. The studies validating anxiety sensitivity were reported by outstanding researchers such as Rolf A. Peterson at George Washington University, Norman Schmidt at Florida State University, Sherry Stewart at Dalhousie University, Steven Taylor at the University of British Columbia, and Michael Zvolensky at the University of Houston. Florida International University Professor Wendy Silverman, and her Ph.D. student and now University of New Orleans Professor Carl Weems, expanded anxiety sensitivity to children. In order to understand how anxiety and fear motivate any individual, we need to know not only how much anxiety the person experiences but also the individual's sensitivity to anxiety (or fear of fear).

In 1995 I was diagnosed with a fatal autoimmune disease and was told I would need a liver transplant. For the rest of my academic career — as of this writing, 18 years — I did not know how long I might live and had the cloud of fatal disease hanging over my head. I was transplanted in 2002 and, although the operation was successful, I experienced life-threatening complications in 2002, 2003, 2007, 2010, and 2011. On two occasions, my doctors told my family I might not make it to morning; on one occasion they said I would die in an hour or so. I lived only because my wife, Maggi, wouldn't let my doctors quit. I have been blessed with life, some very dedicated physicians, and a loving wife and family.

In 1995 I decided to study the meaning of life and to build a psychology based on purpose and values. I executed a series of scientific surveys to identify the basic desires of human nature. As already noted, the results of this research identified 16 basic desires. I then set out to study the implications of the 16 basic desires.

My takeaway from the anxiety sensitivity work McNally and I did was based on both intuition and logic. I surmised that intrinsic motives — which I call "basic desires" to draw attention to how they are experienced subjectively — can be broken down into two components, "what" people want, and "how much" they want. Everyone wants to experience emotional tranquility rather than anxiety. People with high anxiety sensitivity, however, want to experience much more tranquility than do people with low anxiety sensitivity. The intrinsic motive to avoid anxiety breaks down into "what" people want, which is emotional tranquility, and "how much" they want, which varies with sensitivity to anxiety.

I applied this analysis of "what" people want, which is the universal in human motivation, and "how much" they want, which is the particular in human motivation, to each of the 16 basic desires. In the basic desire for curiosity, for example, what people want is understanding, and how much understanding they want depends on the individual's valuation of knowledge. Intrinsic-extrinsic motivation theorists erred when they claimed that everybody enjoys learning. The capacity to enjoy learning isn't infinite. Everybody does not enjoy learning equally, nor does everybody place equal value on intellectual knowledge. Intellectuals place a much higher value on knowledge than practical people do, and this difference in valuation corresponds very closely to differences in motivation for intellectual pursuits.

Shortly before my liver transplant in 2002, at a time when my survival was uncertain, business coaches in Germany asked for my permission to apply the 16 basic desires. This activity eventually gave rise to what is now called "Reiss Profile Europe," which is a training institute located in Cologne, Berlin, and Amsterdam. Success led to other institutes throughout Europe, North America, and Asia. At the time of this writing in the fall of 2012, seven institutes teach professional applications of the 16 basic desires, mostly to clients who work in business but also to people who work in schools, health care, and sports.

Blog B

Three Pillars of Motivational Psychology

In this blog I brief identify what is original and important in the theory of 16 basic desires: (1) the scientific derivation of 16 psychological needs or basic desires; (2) the conceptual platform for connecting motivation and personality; and (3) the conceptual platform for connecting motivation and relationships.

William James and William McDougall, both professors at Harvard during the first years of the last century, put forth a theory of instincts, which they said were a central organizing theme of behavior. They were raked over the coals with criticisms of the concept of "instinct." Psychodynamic theorists, eager to expand on Freud's motivation theory of libido, redefined "instincts" as ego motives. Henry Murray, another Harvard professor, renamed instincts "unconscious needs" and published a story-telling technique, the Thematic Apperception Test (TAT), to assess needs. By the 1950s, motivational psychology was at the center of academic clinical psychology, and the TAT was very widely used.

What happened? Scientific evaluations of the TAT were less than glowing. Leonard Eron and his colleagues authored an influential evaluation that drew negative implications for the scientific status of the TAT. When the TAT became controversial, needs theory gradually declined in influence. Needs theory also was vulnerable to a sharp decline in popularity because it had limited practical implications. The primary application of Murray's needs was clinical diagnosis within the psychodynamic, DSM II model. When the DSM II diagnostic model became obsolete, Murray's needs theory lost influence. Abraham Maslow's theory of a hierarchy of needs appealed to human resource managers and, consequently, found an application in corporate leadership training. For the most part, however, psychologists were clueless on how to apply theories of psychological needs to professional activities.

How clueless? A fellow professor once asked me about my taxonomy of 16 basic desires. As I explained the theory, she became really excited, finally saying, "That is really interesting. Too bad you can't use for it anything."

By 1990, needs theory had become an oldie but goodie, a blast from the past, something nobody paid attention to except when studying history. This seemed to me to be a shame because the basic insight is valid, namely, that there are certain goals (called "needs") that motivate everyone. In the words of behaviorists, some of whom say they don't like concepts like "needs," there are certain stimuli that reinforce everyone. Whether we call them instincts, needs, universal goals, intrinsic motives, or universal reinforcements, they are crucial for understanding people, how we behave in natural environments, and how we relate to each other.

PILLAR I: EMPIRICAL DERIVATION OF NEEDS

I have been trying to rebuild needs theory based on three pillars (or unique ideas). We have reported the first-ever, empirically-derived taxonomy of needs, and in the process we redefined what is and is not included in each need. Our taxonomy of 16 needs includes basic desires for acceptance, curiosity, eating, honor, status, tranquility, and so on. It has about 50% overlap with the lists of needs provided by McDougall, Murray, and others. Because the 16 basic desires are empirically derived and scientifically validated, the theory avoids numerous errors in how psychologists have historically combined motives into needs. The desire to socialize, for example, isn't incompatible with the desire for revenge. Play is about fun, not competence. The desire for wealth falls under a larger need for social status.

PILLAR II: MOTIVATION AND PERSONALITY

Everybody embraces the 16 basic desires, but individuals prioritize them differently. Your prioritization of the 16 basic desires, called a Reiss Profile®, reveals your intrinsic values and personality traits and is a powerful predictor of your behavior. In my book, The Normal Personality, I suggested the specific motives of every personality trait in a dictionary. Ken Olson and his colleagues correlated Reiss Profiles to various personality assessments including the "Big 5".

PILLAR III: MOTIVATION AND RELATIONSHIPS

We articulated the principles of self-hugging and everyday tyranny and then used them to connect motivational needs to various kinds of enduring relationships including parent-child, spouses, supervisor-worker, and colleagues.

PRACTICAL APPLICATIONS

Various individuals have applied the 16 basic desires to school motivation, motivation in business, motivation in sports, motivating healthy behaviors, planning preferred lifestyles for people with intellectual disabilities, conflict resolution, and relationships.

KEY INNOVATION

My work on motivation dates back to 1980 with the start of my research on what I called "anxiety sensitivity," which I published in 1985 with Richard McNally (then a graduate student, now a Harvard University Professor). Over and over critics told us that anxiety sensitivity is superfluous because everybody avoids anxiety. We replied that anxiety motivates some people more than others. As of today, anxiety sensitivity has been validated in more than 1,600 peer-reviewed scientific articles, including two favorable "Psychological Bulletin" summary review articles. The United States Army recently reported that anxiety sensitivity is an early predictor of Post-Traumatic Stress Disorder. In many of these studies anxiety sensitivity is shown to be a predictor of outcome variance that could not be predicted by other measures of anxiety. The Anxiety Sensitivity Index (ASI) questionnaire I wrote in less than an hour has outperformed just about every anxiety scale out there. The construct of tranquility, one of our 16 basic desires, is very closely connected to anxiety sensitivity, and the RMP Tranquility scale includes items from the ASI.

My takeaway from our work on anxiety sensitivity is the importance of the concept of "individual differences in valuations of a universal motive." I learned that many scientists thought this psychological factor is just a trifle; actually, such individual differences can be powerful predictors of real-world behavior. I went from studying an individual difference in a single universal motivator (anxiety) to studying individual differences in 16 universal motivators.

BLESSED WITH WEAK-MINDED CRITICS

It is easy to respond to the most common criticisms of the theory of 16 basic desires. Some say we have "too many" needs. We reply that since astronomers say there are billions and billions of stars, and biologists classify hundreds of species, why are 16 needs too many for a psychologist to handle? Another criticism is that our taxonomy of needs is not scientific because early on we modified it from 15 to 16 basic desires. Does this mean that astronomy is unscientific because it went from nine to eight planets? Is chemistry unscientific because of the many additions over the years to the Periodic Chart of Elements? We published peer-reviewed evidence that our theory of 16 basic desires meets the scientific criteria of measurement reliability, construct validity, concurrent validity, and criterion validity.

Based on a presentation delivered at the World Society of Motivation Scientists and Professionals in Vienna, Austria on October 5, 2011.

Blog C

How to Motivate Someone

It makes no sense to try to motivate another person
by appealing to values he or she does not have. Yet
people try this all the time, because of self-hugging.

To motivate another person, you have to appeal to their values. This may seem straightforward, but it isn't. Too often we try to motivate others by indoctrinating them in our values rather than by appealing to theirs. A classic example of this is the football coach who tells his team that the next game will be a test of their character. We have assessed thousands of athletes and have found that, as a group, they do not care much about their character. We asked, anonymously, questions like, "Agree/disagree: I try to behave in accordance with a Code of Conduct," and many of them responded, "Disagree." It makes no sense for a coach (or anyone else) to try to motivate players by appealing to values they don't have.

People have a natural tendency to think their values are best, not just for themselves, but for everyone. People who discover how great it feels to win think they have learned something about human nature — that winning feels great — when in reality they have learned something about themselves. Individuality is much greater than is commonly supposed. Although competitive people like to win, many others dislike keeping score and, thus, are demotivated by competition.

We have a tendency to try to motivate others by indoctrinating them in our values. Some teachers, for example, believe that everyone is born intellectually curious. Faced with overwhelming evidence that some students are not interested in intellectual pursuits, these educators try anyway to teach these students the joys of intellectual life. They are not appealing to the values of the students but are trying to indoctrinate them in their own values. This doesn't work.

Some hardworking parents try to motivate their laid-back adolescents by telling them how important it is to be an achiever. But laid-back adolescents aren't interested in success; if they were, they wouldn't be so comfortable with their laid-back lifestyle. Instead, they value leisure and work/life balance. If you push them too hard, they quit altogether.

Some employers use bonuses to try to motivate their employees. But only some workers are motivated by extra money. Others are motivated by a need to feel competent, and still others are motivated by a need to feel they are making a contribution to society.

How can you learn the values and goals of someone you might want to motivate? My colleagues and I have administered questionnaires to more than 60,000 people in North America, Europe, and Asia. We have worked with students across the United States, employees here and in Europe, and business executives of major corporations. We have spent almost two decades collecting evidence of 16 psychological needs common to us all and deeply rooted in human nature. These needs are acceptance, curiosity, eating, family, honor, idealism, independence, order, physical activity, power, romance, saving, social contact, status, tranquility, and vengeance. All human motives seem to reduce to these 16 needs or to some combination of them.

Scientific psychologists are finally getting around to understanding motivation. My colleagues and I try to understand people by asking them, "What are your goals? What are you trying to accomplish?" Surprisingly, many psychologists do not ask these questions because they assume that conscious motives are superficial. Instead, they ask, "What happened to you in childhood? How do you feel about your parents?"

We are learning that people are motivated to assert their values. If you want to motivate someone — a loved one, a student, or an employee — you would be wise to focus on what that person cares about.

Blog D

Two Views of Promiscuity

Rollo May was a first-rate therapist who earned a reputation for expressing the existential side of therapy. Here is a blog that contrasts my view with his on the nature of promiscuous behavior. What May and the therapy community view as a lack of human development, I view as the meaning of a person's life. Is promiscuity about mental health, or intrinsically held values?

Promiscuity is a long-standing pattern of behavior of having sex more frequently and with more partners than is normative for the culture. In this blog I will compare two explanations, psychodynamic and motivation analysis. A psychodynamic approach explains behavior based on insights (some say speculations) about the so-called unconscious mind. Motivation analysis explains behavior based on standardized assessments of how an individual values the 16 universal goals that move everybody.

Peggy Guggenheim, the wealthy benefactor and collector of modern art, prided herself on her sexual "vitality" and her "passion." She thought better of people who showed romantic passion than those who showed less "life." She valued romance above nearly everything else. Her strong striving for romance motivated her to have many sexual partners throughout much of her life. When asked, "How many husbands have you had?" she replied, "Do you mean my own, or other people's?" According to her autobiography, where she recorded and probably exaggerated her sexual exploits, she had two real husbands, innumerable lovers, and one great love. She had between 3 and 17 abortions; her biographers differ on the exact number.

Guggenheim had an unhappy childhood. Her parents spent long periods apart. Her mother hired nannies to raise her after her father died in the sinking of the luxury liner Titanic. She inherited wealth and moved to Europe but was forced to return to New York when World War II broke out. While living in New York, she started an influential gallery for modern art and created an important forum for young artists. She "supported three of the most important art movements of the last hundred years: cubism, surrealism, and abstract expressionism."

Psychologists who study the unconscious mind, called psychodynamic theorists, say that promiscuity shows a lack of self-respect. Promiscuous people may be trying to compensate for the love their parents never gave them when they were children. Anton Gill wrote that Peggy Guggenheim used sex to fulfill a need to be loved and to bolster her self-esteem. He further suggested that Guggenheim sought sex with many artists because this gave her an unconscious psychological sense of acquiring their creativity, which she lacked.

According to motivation analysis, promiscuity is motivated by a strong sex drive in combination with a below-average need for honor. People with a strong sex drive are always thinking about romance, which is one of their reasons for being. They are vigilant to sexual cues given off by others. As Katherine Hepburn once said of the great actor John Barrymore, he was utterly incapable of letting a girl walk by without grabbing some part of her anatomy.

One of the most valid principles of motivation theory is that strong drives lead to multiple gratification objects. People with strong appetites eat many different kinds of food. Highly curious people are interested in learning about many different topics. People with a strong need for physical activity play several sports. People with strong parenting instincts have large families. People with a strong need to socialize have many friends. This principle, as explained in my book, The Normal Personality, implies that people with a strong sex drive tend to seek out many partners. Thus promiscuity is easily explained, at least in part, as a strong sex drive.

Now let's compare these two theories to see which one better explains Peggy Guggenheim's promiscuous lifestyle. Psychodynamic theory says that Guggenheim engaged in promiscuous sex to reduce the anxiety associated with her feelings of being unloved. Motivation analysis says that Guggenheim engaged in promiscuous sex to satisfy a voracious appetite. We can scientifically evaluate these theories by studying two groups. Group A might consist of 100 people with a poor self-concept (feelings of being unloved) and an average sex drive. Group B might consist of 100 people with an average self-concept and above average sex drive. I believe that such a study would find Group B to be more promiscuous than Group A. In other words, I believe that sex drive predicts promiscuous behavior better than does self-concept.

According to psychodynamic theory, promiscuity is a superficial life-style. According to motivation analysis, promiscuity is experienced as a meaningful behavior for people who have strong sex drives. The evidence supports motivation analysis. Peggy Guggenheim was proud of her sexual exploits. Indeed, she bragged about her sexual conquests, and she belittled people who weren't promiscuous. Guggenheim kept a diary of her adventures, thus clearly valuing her promiscuous behavior. Since we are a species born to assert our values, Peggy Guggenheim lived in accordance with her values when she slept in bed after bed after bed.

Some experts think there must be more to understanding promiscuity than a strong sex drive and weak traditional morals. Existential psychologist Rollo May, for example, suggested that promiscuity reflects an inability to relate to people except superficially. In his 1969 book Love and Will, May distinguished Eros from libido. Eros is the desire to unite, create, and love a partner; libido is the desire for release. Relationships based on Eros are fulfilling and spiritually satisfying, whereas those based only on sex are purely physical and unfulfilling. May believed that in a purely sexual relationship, it is only a matter of time before the partners experience feelings of emptiness.

Peggy Guggenheim did not consider her promiscuity a venture into emptiness; on the contrary, sex was one of the few things in her life that was meaningful to her. She didn't write a diary of her sexual exploits to reveal existential angst but to brag about her passionate nature; she was asserting the meaning in her life, not lamenting the absence of meaning.

Some experts think it is simplistic or circular reasoning to say that Guggenheim was promiscuous because of a strong sex drive. They assume that "something must be wrong" with people who go from lover to lover without a deeper commitment. They know they would experience promiscuous relationships as meaningless, so they are baffled as to why anybody would embrace such a lifestyle.

I am suggesting the opposite of what experts such as Rollo May say. People like May need a monogamous relationship to experience life as meaningful, but people like Guggenheim find meaning in sexual passion. Rollo May confused individuality with abnormality. He described human nature the way he believed it should be. I am describing the truth about human nature. What is meaningful to one person is meaningless to another. Promiscuity was meaningful to Peggy Guggenheim but meaningless to May; monogamy was meaningful to May but meaningless to Peggy Guggenheim.

BLOG E

What I Learned from Prince Charles

How I came to realize that the need for attention is about social status.

The Royal College of Psychiatry invited me to speak at their annual conference. I visited the United Kingdom for the first time, met many interesting people, toured typical tourist sites, and had my expenses paid. How could I refuse?

Being a curious sort, I asked my hosts why their organization is called the "royal" college of psychiatry, as opposed to the "British" college. Could anybody call themselves "royal?" In America, for example, I could open a hamburger stand and call it the "president's" burgers.

My hosts explained that to call your organization "royal," you had to apply for a charter from the Royal family. Further, a member of the family was assigned to be the patron for the organization. Prince Charles is the patron for the Royal College of Psychiatry, and he flew in via helicopter to speak to the conference.

On the morning of the prince's talk, I arrived at the room early and sat in the second row of seats. I would be only a few feet from the prince when he arrived. "Wow," I am thinking, "this beats going to the U.K. as a tourist. Wait a minute, I will be close to the prince and nobody checked me out." In fact I couldn't see any security officers walking around.

Fifteen minutes before Prince Charles's talk, the nobles entered the room and sat in the first row of chairs. Then the press entered and kneeled on the floor in front of the nobles. I sat right behind the nobles.

Prince Charles entered the room, went to the front, and sat in his chair waiting for the session to begin. I just stared at him. What kind of socks does a prince wear? Look at his shirt! His haircut. Then I realized I was gawking. I looked around the room and observed that most people were gawking. Suddenly it struck me how awkward I would feel if everybody stared at me the way we were staring at Prince Charles. I looked again at the prince and he was taking it in with dignity, as if it were natural that people would stare at him.

That is how I came to realize the primal connection between status and attention. We pay attention to people who have high status, and we ignore those who are low status. By definition, royals are the highest possible social status after the divine. Hence we gawk at royals, and they think it normal that we do so.

Prince Charles gave a very good speech. He suggested that the stigma of mental illness rubs off on the doctors who serve this population. Hence psychiatry is a low-status medical profession. "Good thinking for a prince," I thought to myself.

When the prince completed his talk and the session was wrapping up, a British soldier in uniform told the audience that our luggage had been moved from the hotel's sleeping rooms to the lobby. I went to get my luggage, opened my suitcase, and found a note from the U.K. secret police informing me they had inspected my bag. I guess there was security after all, but it was so good I didn't notice it until they sent me a written note.

Blog F

Myths of Intrinsic and Extrinsic Motivation

I have been a leading critic of the social psychology of intrinsic and extrinsic motivation. Here's why.

What happens when a person is offered an incentive to do something the individual would have done anyway, without incentive? In 1975 Edward Deci, Mark Lepper, and their colleagues proposed that rewards undermine intrinsic motivation. In contrast, Len Sushinsky and I argued that the effects of rewards depend on how you use them. If you reward a person for just spending time in an activity, the person will become bored with the activity. If you reward a person for learning a new skill, however, the person is likely to show greater interest in the activity. We also asserted the significance of the symbolic effects of the reward. When reward symbolizes success, for example, intrinsic interest should be enhanced. We were particularly critical of the social psychology experiments that used single-trial rewards because novel rewards can be distracting.

That was 35 years ago. In the interim many studies have been conducted on intrinsic and extrinsic motivation. To prove that rewards undermine intrinsic interest, researchers needed to demonstrate each of the following: construct validity; reliable measures; experimental controls; and favorable experimental results. Let's see what happened.

I believe that intrinsic-extrinsic motivation is an invalid distinction. I would argue that intrinsic-extrinsic motivation is a modern version of mind-body dualism, such that intrinsic motives (e.g., curiosity, self-determination) are those of the mind, while extrinsic motives (e.g., hunger, sex) are those of the body. In any event, I do not think that motives can be divided into just two types. On the contrary, I think there are 16 intrinsic motives (or "needs") and no extrinsic motives. I have no idea even how to state undermining theory when it is appreciated that any of 16 intrinsic needs can motivate interest in an activity, and any of 16 needs can motivate interest in a reward.

I question the reliability of behavioral measures of intrinsic interest. What activities a child chooses while running around a nursery school may vary from day to day for no particular reason. In any event, I do not recall a study demonstrating the test-retest reliability of the behavioral measure of intrinsic motivation. I believe that measures of self-reported interest are reliable, so if I were to review the literature, I would focus only on the studies with self-report measures.

Further, I think certain interpretations of the behavior measure have led to circularity and self-fulfilling prophecy. Suppose we offer a boy a prize for making a good drawing; the boy draws and gets the prize; and now we observe the boy to see if he continues to draw on his own. If the boy draws little after having earned the prize, undermining theorists would interpret this as evidence of decreased intrinsic motivation. They assume that the child could not have been looking for an incentive and thus was intrinsically interested. However, if the boy draws often after having earned the prize, undermining theorists would not interpret this as evidence of increased intrinsic motivation. They assume that the child was looking for a reward and thus was extrinsically motivated. Less drawing supports undermining theory, but more drawing doesn't contradict undermining theory. This "heads I win, tails you lose" thinking is circular; it biased the publication process by misidentifying disconfirming studies as invalid. Many studies that did not support undermining theory were never published because of this faulty logic applied in the peer-review process.

The undermining studies did not control for the known negative effects of reward. Particularly when rewards are novel — nearly all of the undermining studies used only one trial of reward — they can be distracting, arouse performance anxiety, or even cause doubt that the experimenter will actually give the reward as promised.

Even after setting aside the above issues, meta-reviewers hoping to demonstrate undermining theory still needed to exclude some unfavorable studies to do so. The mentality of "let's include this study in the meta-review, but not that study" went to what I would regard as extremes. Studies that contradicted undermining theory — such as a study I published in the Journal of Personality and Social Psychology in 1975 — were not counted in meta-reviews, while the 1977 study by Smith and Pittman was included as supporting undermining even though this study gave multiple trials of a reward that symbolized failure.

Personally, I object to intrinsic-extrinsic motivation because it offers "one size fits all" solutions for educating children and motivating adults. I believe, for example, that some children thrive with cooperative learning, whereas other children thrive with competitive learning situations. Intrinsic-extrinsic motivation theory, however, wants all children to experience cooperative learning. In the name of self-determination, undermining theorists impose their values on others believing it is for their own good. I think undermining theory could be misused to teach children who are competitive by nature that something is wrong with them for enjoying competition.

Intrinsic-extrinsic motivation has become a dead end. I have seen teachers complain that they can't do anything to help students because "the intrinsic motivation has been beaten out of them." Our schools do not need a theory that can function as an excuse for inaction.

BLOG G

Human Behavior is Purposive

*Almost every psychologist views motivation as psychic energy.
I view motivation as the assertion of core values. We are a species born to assert our values. That need moves and inspires us.*

In 1968 I enrolled at Yale Graduate School to study learning theory and
become a behavior therapist. I spent much of 1969 in Boston as a psychology intern at Harvard Medical School's Department of Neurology, learning
from Dr. Murray Sidman's group. Most days I drove psychoanalyst Dr. Hel-
en Beier to work, and occasionally I had a class with Freudian therapists who
came from Massachusetts Mental Hospital to teach the psychology interns.
At Yale, Professor John Dollard and others taught me about psychoanalysis.
These were brilliant people, and it was hard not to be attracted to some of
the Freudian ideas. Dr. Beier had studied psychoanalysis in Vienna.

Today I reject Freud partially because I disagree with his ideas about motivation. For much of his career he had only one motive, libido, and he tried to explain everything as an effort to "discharge libido," whatever that means. In practice, though, Freud saw sex as an anxiety-ridden drive, and he explained almost everything as an effort to reduce anxiety.

In contrast, I believe there are many different motives/drives/instincts/ goals in human life. Everything cannot be reduced to just the sex drive or just anxiety reduction. Jung and other ego theorists (neo-Freudians) argued that Freud's analysis of motivation is too narrowly focused on sex. Yet Freud stubbornly held to recognizing anxiety reduction as the overarching motive of human behavior.

Some Freudians argued that libido means pleasure, and that Freud's eventual recognition of two overarching instincts (love and aggression) is really a pleasure-pain system of motivation. This is hedonism, or the theory that human beings are motivated to maximize pleasure and to minimize pain.

Philosophers disproved hedonism centuries before the birth of Christ. In his book, History of Western Philosophy, the man who co-demonstrated the logical basis for mathematics, Bertram Russell, dismissed pleasure theory with transparent contempt for its simplicities.

But there is a deeper problem with Freud's constructs of libido and anxiety. Freud opted for a mechanical, cause and effect model of human motivation. He held that motivation is psychic energy. He named the energy libido. Later, behaviorists would embrace the concept of "drive," which is same invalid construct of motivation as psychic energy. Thanks to Freud and early behaviorists, psychologists have spent a century trying to understand why people behave as they do while ignoring human purposeS and paying little attention to human values.

My thesis is that human beings are motivated by purposes and values. The best way to understand people is in terms of their life purposes, goals, and values. This also is the best way to predict how people will behave at work, home, school, or on the athletic field. I reject Freud because he erroneously invented unconscious mechanical psychic forces.

Let me use an analogy of a house. If we were to ask what makes the house function, some might cite the energy source. They would say the events in the house are energized by oil, by natural gas, or maybe by solar. If people were houses, many Freudians would admit that Freud identified too few energy sources for powering the house, but they might say that Freud advanced knowledge by describing the house, its rooms, etc. Freudians think motivation is just one part of an overall theory of the human psyche and far from the most important part. They think that ego psychologists fixed Freudian theory by recognizing a wide range of sources for psychological energy in addition to sex.

In contrast, I think motivation is the assertion of values, not the discharge of psychic energy. Motivation is about purpose, not mechanical cause and effect. *It is the blueprint for the house, not the energy source.* Motivation explains the purpose of the living room, the purpose of the kitchen etc. If you get motivation/purpose wrong, you have little idea why the house was built the way it was.

If you want to understand a person's behavior, you need to determine what the person is trying to accomplish and what the person values. Not what you value, but what the person you are trying to understand values. We have created a powerful method, called the Reiss Motivation Profile, of determining an individual's purposes and values.

PART VI

References

References

Adler, A. (1964). The practice and theory of individual psychology. New York: Harcourt, Brace, Jovanovich. Originally published in 1927.

American Psychiatric Association (1994). Diagnostic and statistical manual of mental disorders (4th ed.). Washington, DC: Author.

Aristotle (1953). The Nichomachean ethics (trans. J. A. K. Thompson). New York: Penguin Books. (Original work created about 330 B.C.).

Atkinson, J. W., & Feather, N.T. (1966). A theory of achievement motivation. New York: John Wiley & Sons.

Aureli, F., & de Waal, F. B. M. (2000). Natural conflict resolution. Berkeley: University of California Press.

Crowne, D. P., & Marlowe, D. (1960). A new scale of social desirability independent of psychopathology. Journal of Consulting Psychology, 24, 349-354.

Darwin, C. (1859). The origin of the species. London: Murray.

Deci, E. L., Koestner, R., & Ryan, R. M. (1999). A meta-analytic review of experiments examining the effects of extrinsic rewards on intrinsic motivation. Psychological Bulletin, 125, 627-668.

Deci, E. L., & Ryan, R. M. (1985). Intrinsic motivation and self-determination in human behavior. New York: Plenum.

Deci, E. L. (1975). Intrinsic motivation. New York: Plenum.

Dunlap, K. (1919). Are there any instincts? Journal of Abnormal Psychology, 14, 307-311.

Dykens, E. M., & Rosner, B. A. (1999). Redefining behavioral phenotypes: Personality-motivation in Williams and Prader-Willi syndromes. American Journal of Mental Retardation, 104, 158-169.

Eisenberger, R., & Cameron, J. (1996). The detrimental effects of reward: Myth or reality. American Psychologist, 51, 1153-1166.

Engel, G., Olson, K. R., & Patrick, C. (2002). The personality of love: Fundamental motives and traits related to components of love. Personality and Individual Differences, 32, 839-853.

Eron, L. D., & Huesmann, L. R. (1990). The stability of aggressive behavior – Even unto the third generation. In M. Lewis and S. M. Miller (Eds.), Handbook of developmental psychology (pp. 147-156). New York: Plenum.

Eysenck, H. J. (1952). The effects of psychotherapy: An evaluation. Journal of Consulting Psychology, 16, 319-324.

Filson, J. (2010). The adventures of colonel Daniel Boone. New York: Cosimo Classics.

Freud. S. (1963). Introductory lectures on psychoanalysis. London: Hogarth Press. (Original work published in 1916).

Gill, A. (2002). Art lover: A biography of Peggy Guggenheim. New York: Harper Collins.

Havercamp, S.H., & Reiss, S. (2004). A comprehensive assessment of human striving: Reliability and validity of the Reiss Profile. Journal of Personality Assessment, 81, 123-132.

lson, K. (2007). Research on fundamental motives. In L. Brown (Ed.), Psychology of motivation (pp. 1-3). Hauppauge, NY: Nova Science Publishers.

Jackson, D. N. (1984). Personality Research Form manual. Port Huron, MI: Research Psychologists Press.

James, W. (1918). The principles of psychology (Vol. 2). New York: Dover. (Original work published in 1890).

Judah, S. M. (2006). Staying together when an affair pulls you apart. Downers Grove, IL: IVP Books.

Jung, C. (1923). Psychological types. New York: Harcourt.

Kavanaugh, P., & Reiss, S. (2001). Why high school students get poor grades. Unpublished manuscript, IDS Publishing Corporation.

Lecavalier, L., & Tasse, M. J. (2002). Sensitivity theory of motivation and psychopathology: An exploratory study. American Journal of Mental Retardation, 107, 105-115.

Maller, R., & Reiss, S. (1992). Anxiety sensitivity in 1984 and panic attacks in 1987. Journal of Anxiety Disorders, 6, 241-247.

Mandel, H. P., & Marcus, S. I. (1995). "Could do better": Why children underachieve and what to do about it. New York: J. Wiley.

Maslow, A. H. (1954). Motivation and personality. New York: Harper & Row.

Maslow, A. H. (1943). A theory of motivation. Psychological Review, 50, 370-396.

McClelland, D.C. (1961). The achieving society. Princeton, NJ: Van Nostrand.

McDougall, W. (2003). An introduction to social psychology. Mineola, NY: Dover. (Originally published in 1908).

Mengel, T. (2012). High potential can be deceiving – Utilizing the Reiss Motivation Profile® in HR and leadership development. FMI Journal, 10-12.

Mengel, T. (2012). Leading with 'emotional' intelligence – Existential and motivational analysis in leadership and leadership development. Journal on Educational Psychology, 5, 17-25.

Murray, H. A. (1943). Thematic Apperception Test. Cambridge, MA: Harvard University Press.

Murray, H. A. (1938). Explorations in personality: A clinical and experimental study of fifty men of college age. New York: Oxford University Press.

Myers, I.B., & McCaulley, M.H. (1985). Manual, a guide to the development and use of the Myers-Briggs Type Indicator. Palo Alto, CA: Consulting Psychological Press.

Olson, K., & Chapin. B. (2007). Relations of fundamental motives and psychological needs to well-being and intrinsic motivation. In P. Zelick (Ed.), Issues in the psychology of motivation (pp. 232-243. Hauppauge, NY: Nova Science Publishers.

Olson. K. & Weber, D. (2004). Relations between Big Five traits and fundamental motives. Psychological Reports, 97, 795-802.

Plato (1966). The Republic of Plato. New York: Oxford University Press. Translated by F. M. Cornford. (Originally written in about 360 B.C.)

Ramsay, G. (1843). An inquiry into the principle of human happiness and human duty. London: William Pickering.

Reiss, S. (2010). Human needs and intellectual disabilities. Kingston, NY: NADD.

Reiss, S. (2005a). Extrinsic and intrinsic motivation at 30: Unresolved scientific issues. Behavior Analyst, 28, 1-14.

Reiss, S. (2005b). Why people become organ donors. Paper presented at the annual meeting of the American Public Health Association in New Orleans.

Reiss, S. (2004a). Multifaceted nature of intrinsic motivation: The theory of 16 basic desires. Review of General Psychology, 8, 179-193.

Reiss, S. (2004b). The 16 strivings for God. Zygon, 39, 303-320.

Reiss, S. (2000). Who Am I? The 16 basic desires that motivate our actions and define our personalities. New York: Tarcher/Putnum.

Reiss, S. & Havercamp, S.M. (2005). Motivation in a developmental context: Test of Maslow's theory of self-actualization. Journal of Humanistic Psychology, 45, 41-53.

Reiss, S., & Havercamp, S.M. (1998). Toward a comprehensive assessment of fundamental motivation. Psychological Assessment, 10, 97-106.

Reiss, S., & McNally, R.J. (1985). Expectancy model of fear. In S. Reiss & R.R. Bootzin (Eds.), Theoretical issues in behavior therapy. New York: Academic Press, 107-121.

Reiss, S., Peterson, R.A., Gursky, D.M., & McNally, R.J. (1986). Anxiety sensitivity, anxiety frequency, and the prediction of fearfulness. Behavior Research and Therapy, 24, 1-8.

Reiss, S., & Sushinsky, L.W. (1975). Overjustification, competing responses, and the acquisition of intrinsic interest. Journal of Personality and Social Psychology, 31, 1116-1125.

Reiss, S. & Wiltz, J. (2004). Why people watch reality TV? Media Psychology, 6, 363-378.

Reiss, S., Wiltz, J., & Sherman, M. (2001). Trait motivational correlates of athleticism. Journal of Personality and Individual Differences, 30, 1139-1145.

Russell, B. (1972). A history of western philosophy. New York: Simon & Shuster. (Originally published in 1945.)

Schwartz, S. H. (1994). Are there universal aspects in the structure and contents of human values? Journal of Social Issues, 50, 19-45.

Takakuwa, M., & Wakabayashi, M. (1999, personal communication). Unpublished factor study of Japanese translation of the Reiss Motivation Profile® with Japanese college students.

Ullmann, L. P., & Krasner, L. (Eds., 1965). Case studies in behavior modification. New York: Holt.

Weiner, B. (1995). Intrinsic motivation. In A. Manstead, M. Hewstone, S. Fiske, M. Hoggs, H. Reis, & G. Samin (Eds.) The Blackwell encyclopedia of social psychology. Cambridge, UK: Blackwell.

White, R. W. (1959). Motivation reconsidered: The concept of competence. Psychological Review, 66, 297-333.

Wiltz, J., & Reiss, S. (2003). Compatibility of housemates with mental retardation. <u>American Journal of Mental Retardation</u>, <u>108</u>, 173-180.

Zubin, J., Eron, L. D., & Schumer, F. (1965). <u>An experimental approach to projective techniques</u>. New York: Wiley.

About the Author

STEVEN REISS is a retired tenured Professor of Psychology living in Columbus, Ohio. He was educated at Dartmouth College (A.B.) and Yale University (Ph.D.) and completed a clinical psychology internship at Harvard Medical School. He is a Senior Fellow of Dartmouth College and a Fellow of both the American Psychological Association and the American Association on Intellectual Disabilities. He taught at The Ohio State University and the University of Illinois at Chicago.

In a series of scientific studies, Steven Reiss identified 16 basic desires of human nature. This research was reported in numerous newspapers of record worldwide in addition to scientific journals of the highest quality. He is the author of the Reiss Motivation Profile ®(RMP), a widely used standardized psychological assessment of what motivates someone. His methods are taught through a worldwide network of training institutes. The RMP has many applications including self-discovery; motivating workforce; human resources; leadership training; conflict resolution; motivating students; world-class athletics (Olympic teams); counseling; coaching; relationships; marketing; faith-based counseling; and wellness. The instrument has been translated into most European languages as well as an increasing number of Asian languages.

In 1985 Steven Reiss proposed (with Richard McNally) the concept of anxiety sensitivity, which has been validated in more than 1,600 peer-reviewed studies. He is the author of the Anxiety Sensitivity Index, which is a standardized psychological assessment widely used throughout the world to study and diagnose Panic Disorder and Post-Traumatic Stress Disorder.

In the 1980s and 1990s Steven Reiss conducted extensive research on the mental health aspects of intellectual disabilities, or the co-occurrence of psychiatric disorders and developmental disabilities. This work was recognized with five national awards and was cited to help justify hundreds of new psychiatric and psychological clinics in North America and Europe. In 1988 he authored the Reiss Screen for Maladaptive Behavior, a standardized assessment tool that has been used extensively to screen for the need for psychiatric services. He gave an invited presentation before the Civil Rights Division of the United States Department of Justice in addition to three invited presentations at the National Institutes of Health. In 1987 Steven Reiss organized the first-ever international research conference on the mental health aspects of intellectual disabilities. The Director of the National Institute of Mental Health convened an ad hoc review panel specifically to fast track the funding for this conference. Steven Reiss received three awards for volunteer efforts serving people with disabilities.

In 1995 Steven Reiss was diagnosed with a life-threatening autoimmune disease, and in 2002 he received a liver transplant at The Ohio State University Medical Center. With Linda Jones he started a national program to improve access to organ transplantation for people with intellectual disabilities. This work has been reported in hundreds of newspapers and was cited in a number of recent nationally publicized cases. Since 1995 Steven Reiss has worked with recurrent, life-threatening illnesses.

In 2008 Steven Reiss founded the World Society of Motivation Scientists and Professionals, a nonprofit organization.

Steven Reiss's theory of religion builds on and extends William James's observation that different types of people respond to different aspects of religion. The publication of this theory in academic journals, notably Zygon, was reported in the Chronicle of Higher Education and in the Washington Post. Steven Reiss believes that religious experiences are about the meaning of life and cannot be reduced to just one or two themes – such as morality, community, or fear of death – as some previous scholars asserted.

According to the Social Science Citation Index, other psychologists and scholars have cited Reiss's research frequently.

In 1971 Steven Reiss married Maggi Musico. Maggi, a graduate of Smith College (A.B.) and the University of Illinois at Chicago (M.A.) is a school psychologist and president of IDS Publishing Corporation, which was founded in 1987. They have two adult children: Michael, who is a statistician, and Benjamin, who is a physician. In 2012 Michael married Kristen Lambert, an architect.